CURRENT ISSUES BIBLE STUDY SERIES

The Bible:

Irrelevant or Invaluable

CHRISTIANITY TODAY
INTERNATIONAL

THOMAS NELSON
Since 1798

NASHVILLE DALLAS MEXICO CITY RIO DE JANEIRO BEIJING

Current Issues Bible Study Series: The Bible

Editor: Kelli B. Trujillo
Development Editors: Kelli B. Trujillo and Roxanne Wieman
Associate Editor: JoHannah Reardon
Page Designer: Robin Crosslin

ISBN 13: 978-1-4185-3410-3

Printed in the United States of America
08 09 10 11 12 RRD 5 4 3 2 1

CONTENTS

CONTRIBUTING WRITERS

D. Jeffrey Bingham is Department Chair and Professor of Theological Studies at Dallas Theological Seminary and is the author of many books including *Pocket History of the Church.*

Chris Blumhofer was associate editor of BuildingChurchLeaders.com, a Christianity Today International website devoted to equipping church leaders. He is now pursuing his Master of Divinity degree at Duke.

Wayne Brouwer is a visiting professor of biblical studies at Hope College and is the author of many books and articles.

Elesha Coffman is a graduate student in religion at Duke University. She was formerly the managing editor of *Christian History* magazine.

Gary A. Gilles is adjunct instructor at Trinity International University, editor of *Chicago Caregiver* magazine, a freelance writer, and a licensed clinical professional counselor.

Dr. Ronald Habermas is professor and chair of biblical studies and Christian formation at John Brown University. He is the author of many journal articles and several books including *The Complete Disciple: A Model for Cultivating God's Image in Us* (Chariot Victor) and *Introduction to Christian Education and Formation: A Lifelong Plan for Christ-Centered Restoration* (Zondervan).

Richard A. Kauffman is a former associate editor of *Christianity Today* and is now senior editor at *The Christian Century*.

Scot McKnight is professor of religious studies at North Park University in Chicago and the author many books, including *The Blue Parakeet: Rethinking How You Read the Bible* (Zondervan, 2008). You can join Scot in conversation at www.jesuscreed.org.

J. I. Packer is a senior editor of CT and is the Board of Governors' Professor of Theology at Regent College in Vancouver. He is the author of multiple books including his seminal work *Knowing God.*

John Stek served as a professor of Old Testament, Calvin Theological Seminary, Grand Rapids, Michigan, for thirty years. He was a member of the translation committee for the New International Version and an associate editor of The NIV Study Bible.

Kelli B. Trujillo is an editor, author, and adult ministry leader at her church in Indianapolis.

Raymond C. Van Leeuwen is professor of Biblical Studies at Eastern College in St. Davids, Pennsylvania. He is indebted to Dr. Barrie Evans of Kent, England, for his long-standing help in linguistics. A more extensive treatment of this topic appears in the book *After Pentecost* (Zondervan).

Ben Witherington III is professor of New Testament at Asbury Theological Seminary and author of many books, including *What Have They Done with Jesus?*

INTRODUCTION

The B-I-B-L-E, now that's the book for me!

You've probably found yourself smiling along as kids in your church have sung this song because it's a truth you heartily embrace: God's Word is central to your life.

But many in our culture question the Bible's validity. Isn't it just a collection of flawed, ancient texts? Wasn't it assembled by power-hungry men who purposefully excluded other equally valid "gospels"? After being transmitted across centuries and various languages, is the Bible we have today really an equal to the original texts? And is it even reasonable to consider a book that's so old as having any bearing on modern issues?

As we interact with non-Christian friends or as we dig into Scripture and are faced with some of these complex questions ourselves, we realize that it's critical to move beyond simple childhood choruses and reflect more deeply on the Bible's history, its authority, and its relevance in today's world.

This *Current Issues Bible Study* guide is designed to facilitate lively and engaging discussion on various facets of this topic and how it connects to our lives as Jesus's followers. As you learn more about the Bible together, we hope this *Current Issues Bible Study* will help you grow closer as a group and challenge you in ways you may not expect.

For Small Groups

These studies are designed to be used in small groups—communities of people with a commitment to and connection with each other. Whether you're an existing small group or you're just planning to meet for the next eight weeks, this resource will help you deepen your personal faith and grow closer with each other.

On SmallGroups.com, you'll find everything you need to successfully run a small-groups ministry. The insightful, free articles and theme-specific downloads provide expert training. The reproducible curriculum courses bring thought leaders from across the world into your group's discussion at a fraction of the price. And the revolutionary SmallGroupsConnect social network will help keep your group organized and connected 24/7.

Christianity Today Articles

Each study session begins with one or two thought-provoking articles from *Christianity Today* or one of its sister publications. These articles are meant to help you dive deeply into the topic and engage with a variety of thoughts and opinions. Be sure to read the articles before you arrive to your small group meeting; the time you invest on the front end will greatly enrich your group's discussion. As you read, you may find the articles persuasive and agree heartily with their conclusions; other times you may disagree with the claims of an article, but that's great too. We want these articles to serve as a springboard for lively discussion, so differences in opinion are welcome. For more insightful articles from *Christianity Today* magazine, visit http://www.ctlibrary.com/ and subscribe now.

Timing

These studies are designed to be flexible, with plenty of discussion, activities, and prayer time to fill a full small group meeting. If you'd like, you can zero in on a few questions or teaching points and discuss them in greater depth, or you can aim to spend a few minutes on each question of a given session. Be sure to manage your time so that you're able to spend time on the "Going Forward" questions and prayer time at the end of each study.

Ground Rules

True spiritual growth happens in the context of a vibrant Christian community. To establish that type of community in your small group, we recommend a few *ground rules.*

- *Guarantee confidentiality*. Promise together that whatever is said in the context of your small group meeting is kept there. This sense of trust and safety will enable you to more honestly share your spiritual struggles.

- *Participate—with balance.* We all have different personalities. Some of us like to talk . . . a lot. Others of us prefer to be quiet. But for this study to truly benefit your group, everyone needs to participate. Make it a personal goal to answer (aloud) at least half of the discussion questions in a given session. This will allow space for others to talk (lest you dominate discussion too much) but will also guarantee your own contribution is made to the discussion (from which other group members will benefit).
- *Be an attentive listener—to each other and to God.* As you read Scripture and discuss these important issues, focus with care and love on the other members of your group. These questions are designed to be open-ended and to allow for a diversity of opinion. Be gracious toward others who express views that are different than your own. And even more important, prayerfully remain attentive to the presence of God speaking to and guiding your group through the Holy Spirit.

It is our prayer that this *Current Issues Bible Study* will change the lives of your group members as you seek to integrate your faith into the biblical issues you face every day. May the Holy Spirit work in and through your group as you challenge and encourage each other in spiritual growth.

How should we interpret ancient texts in modern times?

SCRIPTURE FOCUS

- Deuteronomy 11:18–21
- Hebrews 4:12–13
- Matthew 5:17–20

A BIBLE FOR THE TWENTY-FIRST CENTURY

■

In 2007, A. J. Jacobs made waves with his book *The Year of Living Biblically*. As the title suggests, Jacobs's book catalogues his efforts to follow literally the commands of the Bible for a full year. The resulting memoir was well received for its candor, its humor, and, in many places, its reverence.

Yet while it gathered praise from some, *The Year of Living Biblically* served as a platform for others to air their grievances with the Bible for commandments that seem "absurd," "irrelevant," or just "impossible."

Even among Christians these sentiments exist, much of the skepticism being rooted in questions like "Is it even possible for the Bible to be relevant to Christians today?"

Using Scot McKnight's article "The Hermeneutics Quiz" from *Leadership* journal, we're going to explore some initial steps we can take to better understand the Bible.

Before You Meet

Read "The Hermeneutics Quiz" by Scot McKnight from *Leadership* journal.

THE HERMENEUTICS QUIZ

Your biblical blind spots and what you tend not to see.

by Scot McKnight

For some reason of late, I have become fascinated with the portions of the Bible we don't tend to read, passages like the story of Jephthah. Or how God was on the verge of killing Moses for not circumcising his son, and his wife stepped in, did what needed to be done, and tossed the foreskin at Moses's feet, and God let him alone.

I'm curious why one of my friends dismisses the Friday-evening-to-Saturday-evening Sabbath observance as "not for us today" but insists that capital punishment can't be dismissed because it's in the Old Testament.

I have become fascinated with what goes on in our heads and our minds and our traditions (and the latter is far more significant than many of us recognize) in making decisions like this.

What decisions? Which passages not to read as normative. The passages we tend not to read at all.

If we're all subject to selective perception, at least to some degree, it's important to recognize what we tend to miss or gloss over, especially if we're church leaders.

This quiz is designed to surface the decisions we make, perhaps without thinking about them, and about how we both read our Bible and don't read our Bible. Some will want to quibble with distinctions or agree with more than one answer. No test like this can reveal all the nuances needed, but broad answers are enough to raise the key issues. On a scale of 1-5, mark the answer that best fits your approach to reading the Bible. (If you fall between response 1 and response 3, give yourself a 2; if you fall between response 3 and response 5, give yourself a 4.) Your score will reveal where you land on our hermeneutical scale.

THE HERMENEUTICS QUIZ

Circle your answers.

1) The Bible is:

√1. God's inspired words in confluence with the authors.

3. God's inspired words that arise out of a community and then are written down by an author.

5. Words of an author who speaks out of a community's tradition, but which sacramentally lead us to God.

2) The Bible is:

1. God's exact words for all time.

√3. God's message (instead of exact words) for all time.

5. God's words and message for that time that need interpretation and contextualization to be lived today.

3) The Bible's words are:

√1. Inerrant on everything.

3. Inerrant on only matters of faith and practice.

5. Not defined by inerrancy or errancy, which are modernistic categories.

4) The commands in the Old Testament to destroy a village, including women and children, are:

√1. Justifiable judgment against sinful, pagan, immoral peoples.

3. God's ways in the days of the Judges (etc.): they are primitive words but people's understanding as divine words for that day.

5. A barbaric form of war in a primitive society and I wish they weren't in the Bible.

5) The story of Hosea (the prophet) and Gomer (his wife) is:

√ 1. A graphic reality that speaks of God's faithfulness and Israel's infidelity.

3. A parable (since, for example, God would never ask a prophet to marry a prostitute).

5. An unfortunate image of an ancient prophet that stereotypes women and too easily justifies violence against women.

6) The command of Jesus to wash feet is:

√ 1. To be taken literally, despite near universal neglect in the church.

3. A first century observance to be practiced today in other ways.

5. An ancient custom with no real implication for our world.

7) The gift of prophecy is:

√ 1. Timeless, despite lack of attention in the church today.

3. An ancient form of communication that is seen today in proclaiming scriptural truths.

5. No longer needed, dramatically different from today's preaching.

8) Homosexuality's prohibitions in the Bible are:

√ 1. Permanent prohibitions reflecting God's will.

3. Culturally shaped, still normative, but demanding greater sensitivity today.

5. A purity-code violation that has been eliminated by Christ.

9) The unity of the Bible is:

√ 1. God's systematic truth that can be discerned by careful study of the Bible.

3. The gospel call to living by faith that is expressed in a variety of ways by different authors in the Bible.

5. Not found by imposing on the integrity of each author in the Bible to conform to overarching systems; the unity is in the God who speaks to us today through the Word.

10) The Holy Spirit's role in interpretation is:

√1. To guide the individual regardless of what others say.

3. To guide the individual in tandem/conversation with the church.

5. To guide the community that can instruct the individual.

11) The injunctions upon women in 1 Timothy 2:9-15 are:

1. Timeless truths and normative for today.

√3. Culturally shaped but, with proper interpretation and transfer, for today; e.g., we can learn from how Paul addressed a situation with uninstructed women in Ephesus.

5. Needed for early Christians, bound in the first century, but not for today.

12) Careful interpretation of the Bible is:

√1. Objective, rational, universal, timeless.

3. Dialectical, relational, culturally shaped, timely.

5. Subjective, personal, culturally bound, time specific.

13) The context for reading the Bible is:

1. The individual's sole responsibility.

3. The individual in conversation and respect for Church traditions.

√ 5. The confessional statement of one's community of faith.

14) Discerning the historical context of a passage is:

1. Unimportant since God speaks directly to me.

√ 3. Often and sometimes significant in order to grasp meaning.

5. Necessary and dangerous to avoid in reading the Bible.

15) The Bible:

1. Can be examined and understood without bias.
3. Can be understood but with bias.
✓5. Can be partially understood by a reader with bias.

16) Capital punishment:

1. Should be practiced today because the Bible teaches it.
✓3. Should be examined carefully to determine if it is the best option today; some instances of capital punishment in the Bible are no longer advisable.
5. As delineated in the Bible pertains to ancient Israel; such practices are no longer useful and should be universally banned.

17) Tattoos:

1. Are forbidden because of Leviticus 19:28.
✓3. Are forbidden in Leviticus as idolatrous marks, which we know from study of the ancient Near East.
5. Are permissible, because the purity codes are not for Christians today.

18) The requirement of the Jerusalem Council (Acts 15:29) not to eat any meat improperly killed (strangled instead of having the blood drained properly):

1. Is a permanent commandment for all Christians today.
3. Is for Jewish Christians only.
✓5. Is a temporary custom for first-century Jewish Christians, and is no longer a concern for Christians.

19) Adultery:

1. Deserves the death penalty, as stated in the Old Testament.
✓3. Was not punished by death when Jesus confronted it, and therefore death is not a Christian punishment.

5. Adultery and divorce were governed by Old Testament laws from a primitive culture, very different from our own; just as these concepts developed within Bible times, our understanding of proper punishment has been improved.

20) Sabbath:

1. Was never eliminated by New Testament writers and should be practiced by Christians (on Saturday).
3. Developed into a Sunday worship observance for Christians, and Christians should not work on that day.
√5. Turned into Sunday for Christians, who need to worship together (on the weekend, at least) and can work if they think they need to.

Results:

Add up your points for each question (1-5). (If you fall between answer 1 and 3, give yourself a 2. If you fall between answer 3 and 5, give yourself a 4.)

Total: 56

If you scored **20 to 52**, you are a "conservative" when it comes to hermeneutics.

If you scored **53 to 65**, you are a "moderate" when it comes to hermeneutics.

If you scored **66 to 100**, you are a "progressive" when it comes to hermeneutics.

Your score, our findings

I ran this test with about twenty pastors, professors, and former students. No one answered every question with "1" and no one answered every question with "5." I was surprised by the low score of an emergent friend and the high score of a professor at a very conservative Christian college. Some answer progressively on one controversial issue (say, women in ministry), while answering conservatively on others (homosexuality, for example).

The fodder for conversation is how we discern when to be a "1," when to be a "3," and when to be a "5." Broadly speaking, there are three groups here.

First, the **conservative** hermeneutic group scores 52 or lower. The strength of this view is its emphasis on the authority, ongoing and normative authority, of all of Scripture. It tends to operate with the line many of us learned in Sunday school: "If the Bible says it, that settles it." Such persons let the Bible challenge them with full force. Literal readings lead to rather literal applications. Most of the time.

The problem, of course, is that very few people are completely consistent here. At times one suspects something other than strict interpretation is going on when the conservative is willing to appeal to history to suspend the commandment to observe a Saturday Sabbath but does not to appeal to history on other issues (e.g., capital punishment or homosexuality).

The **moderate** hermeneutic might be seen as the voice of reason and open-mindedness. Moderates generally score between 53 to 65. Many are conservative on some issues and progressive on others. It intrigues that conservatives tend to be progressive on the same issues, while progressives tend to be conservative on the same issues. Nonetheless, moderates have a flexible hermeneutic that gives them the freedom to pick and choose on which issues they will be progressive or conservative. For that reason, moderates are more open to the charge of inconsistency. What impresses me most about moderates are the struggles they endure to render judgments on hermeneutical issues.

The **progressive** is not always progressive. Those who score 66 or more can be seen as leaning toward the progressive side, but the difference between a 66 and 92 is dramatic. Still, the progressive tends to see the Bible as historically shaped and culturally conditioned, and yet most still consider it the Word of God for today. Following a progressive hermeneutic, for the Word to speak in our day, one must interpret what the Bible said in its day and discern its pattern for revelation in order to apply it to our world. The strength, as with the moderate but even more so, is the challenge to examine what the Bible said in its day, and this means the progressives tend to be historians. But the problems for the progressives are predictable: Will the Bible's so-called "plain meaning" be given its due and authoritative force to challenge our world? Or will the Bible be swallowed by a quest to find modern analogies that sometimes minimize what the text clearly says?

Wherever you land on this scale, it is my hope we all will engage the seriousness of how we read the Bible—and don't read the Bible.

Scot McKnight is professor of religious studies at North Park University in Chicago and the author of many books. You can join Scot in conversation at www.jesuscreed.org. "The Hermeneutics Quiz" was first published in Leadership *journal and www.BuildingChurchLeaders.com on February 25, 2008. It is also included in* The Blue Parakeet: Rethinking How You Read the Bible, © *Scot McKnight, used by permission of Zondervan. All rights reserved.*

■ Open Up

Select one of these activities to launch your discussion time.

Option 1

Discuss these icebreaker questions:

- What do you think of A.J. Jacobs's effort to follow literally the commands of the Bible for one year? Are his efforts admirable? Misguided? Ridiculous?
- Have you ever been confounded by the Bible's stance on an issue—divorce, gender roles, capital punishment, or something else? Share with the group your experience working through the disconnect between our twenty-first-century logic and the logic of Scripture.

Option 2

Review the "Hermeneutics Quiz" self-test that you took in preparation for this study. Share your score with the rest of your group, then talk about these questions.

- What score did you receive? Did it surprise you in any way?
- Were there any questions on which you ranked noticeably different from the others? (For example, responding as "progressive," a 5, when you trended toward "conservative" answer 1.)
- Do you agree with your quiz results? Does it line up with how you view the way you relate to Scripture?

The Issue

In his book *Orthodoxy,* G. K. Chesterton wrote, "The Christian ideal has not been tried and found wanting; it has been found difficult and left untried." Those words aptly describe the struggles we face when we pick up our Bibles. We believe what Scripture says about itself—that it is living and active (Hebrews 4:12), that it is God-breathed (2 Timothy 3:16), that it is a light to our paths (Psalm 119:105). But then we run up against passages that don't make sense, or we encounter a difficult situation in life and struggle to reconcile our situation with Scripture.

- What's a passage, biblical teaching, or book of the Bible that you've found difficult to understand or apply? Brainstorm several challenging passages together.

For some, this is a brick wall. But understanding what the Bible says on an issue shouldn't require everyone to develop skills in ancient languages, distant cultures, and complicated theology.

The Bible is God's Word. God wants his people to know it, to understand it, and to apply it. But he never promises to make biblical interpretation easy. In fact, as we explore below, we'll find that understanding God's Word comes as the result of finely tuned hearts and habits, and deep faith in the One who promises that his words will accomplish their work.

Reflect

The first two passages in this study employ a great deal of imagery. Read Deuteronomy 11:18–21 and Hebrews 4:12–13; as you do, make a note of each image that is set forth and think about the effect of placing so many images into such a small amount of space. What is the cumulative effect—the message communicated—when you consider the imagery in these passages?

Let's Explore

Recognize how you approach the Bible.

Every Bible reader—from the faithful Sunday school teacher to the highly trained theologian—comes to the Bible from a certain perspective. Our perspectives cause us to gravitate toward certain passages and strain away from others. Scot McKnight calls this "selective perception."

- Have you ever disagreed with another Christian about whether or not a command in Scripture was applicable to believers today? Describe your experience.

- What events or experiences shape your perspective? If your situation changed (say, for example, that you were considerably richer or poorer) how might the way you read the Bible shift? Can you pick out any possible examples from your responses on "The Hermeneutics Quiz" self test?

Try an old-school approach.

It's easy to feel isolated and discouraged when thinking about the power of Scripture in comparison to the puniness of our understanding. Some commands seem straightforward, but when a real-life situation creeps up, their application falls somewhere between difficult and incomprehensible.

In an interview called "The Habits of Highly Effective Bible Readers" from *Christian History and Biography* magazine, Christopher Hall says that the best way to get through the struggles we face is to interpret the Bible in light of the past. Specifically, by looking back to the practices of the church fathers—biblical interpreters from the second through the fifth centuries who read and understood their Bibles—as they were taught by the apostles and the generations immediately after them.

Of course, the twenty-first century is very different from the fifth, and early church leaders probably suffered from at least a little bit of their own "selective perception." At the end of his article, Hall says there are five practices we can do to read the Bible more like the fathers, whether or not we adapt all their interpretations. Hall lists: (1) involvement in the life of the church; (2) understanding church history; (3) a big-picture view of the Bible; (4) a "finely-tuned heart"; and (5) an active life of prayer.

- How might reading the Bible while practicing these steps have a big impact on the way you understand the Bible—even the confusing passages?

- Refer back to the passages from Deuteronomy and Hebrews. How do they relate to the practices outlined above?

- Would you be more inclined to trust an interpretation that was arrived at through these five steps? Why or why not?

- Which of the five steps above do you feel the least equipped to move forward in? Which do you feel the most equipped for? Explain.

Read in faith.

Now read Matthew 5:17–20.

In this passage from the Sermon on the Mount, Jesus is explaining what his relationship is to the Old Testament Law and Prophets. If Jesus were simply a first-century rabbi, we might expect him to say that he did not come to abolish the Law and Prophets, but to explain or elucidate them. Jesus makes two shocking statements instead: (1) he claims that he fulfills them, and (2) he claims that nothing from the Law or Prophets can be set aside.

- What's the impact of Matthew 5:17–20 for how we approach the Bible? How does Jesus's statement relate to passages of Scripture that many of us avoid or find confusing?

- How has your faith in Christ helped you understand other passages of Scripture (outside of the gospels)? Give examples of biblical passages or stories that are elucidated by your understanding of God's "big story" of redemption through Christ.

Going Forward

Speaking of how the Bible shaped the lives of the Hebrew people, John Ortberg writes:

> The book is what shaped them and held them together. The book started every morning: "Hear O Israel, the Lord our God, the Lord is One." The book didn't say, "O Israel, think for yourselves. Follow your bliss. Go with your gut." It just said, *Hear*. It was the source of all wisdom, the guidance for all problems, the authoritative appeal in every debate. The rabbis often disagreed over what it *meant*. But everybody understood its *status*. It was the last word. They never got over this awe that in this book God has spoken—*"What advantage is there, then, of being a Jew? Much in every way! First of all, they have been entrusted with the very words of God" (Rom. 3:1).*
>
> They had the book. And now this book, with some significant additions, has become our book. (*Leadership* Journal, Winter 2008)

- Consider again the thought that began this study: "The Christian ideal has not been tried and found wanting; it has been found difficult and left untried." What are some practical ways that we can help each other apply the lessons of this study?

Pray together, asking God for wisdom and discernment as you continue to study God's Word together.

Notes

Are the words of the Bible really the words of God?

SCRIPTURE FOCUS

- Deuteronomy 4:1–14
- John 8:12–26
- 2 Timothy 3:14–17
- Hebrews 1:1–2

SESSION 2

CAN I TRUST THE BIBLE?

Some of us can go years without noticing those little footnotes in our Bibles—the tiny print that inform us of segments of verses (or even entire paragraphs) that aren't included in the earliest manuscripts of Scripture. But then along comes a non-Christian friend who claims the Bible is full of holes and mistakes, pointing out several of these mysterious footnotes to us. How can we respond? Does this mean there are *mistakes* in Scripture? What about inerrancy? Can we trust in documents that have been compiled, copied and recopied, and passed down over thousands of years? And what can we say to friends who question the Bible's reliability?

In this study we'll explore J. I. Packer's response to questions about the Bible's inerrancy and its importance in our lives today. We'll look at some of the problematic texts in Scripture and will draw from the Bible and church history to help us defend the Bible from critics and deepen our own understanding of Christianity's sacred text.

Before You Meet

Read "Text Criticism and Inerrancy" from *Christianity Today*.

TEXT CRITICISM AND INERRANCY

Answered by J. I. Packer

How can I reconcile my belief in the inerrancy of Scripture with comments in Bible translations that state that a particular verse is not "in better manuscripts"?

—Carol Stanley, Manchester, New Hampshire

The answer to this question parallels that of Charles Spurgeon who, when asked to reconcile human freedom with divine predestination, said, "I never reconcile friends." He maintained that the two realities fit together.

The New Testament books first circulated in hand-copied form, and hand-copying by monks went on till Gutenberg invented the printing press in the fifteenth century. Anyone who has copied by hand knows how easily letters, words, and even whole lines get dropped out or repeated. The New Testament manuscript tradition was not exempt from this.

Also, it is clear that some copyists facing what they thought were miscopyings made what they thought were corrections. Some of these copyists added in the margin, amplifying words and sentences that the next copyist put into the text itself, thinking that was where they belonged. Because the copying was done reverently and with professional care, manuscripts vary little overall, except for the occasional slip of this kind. Manuscript comparison reveals many passages that clearly need correcting at this level of detail.

The King James Version New Testament was translated from the "received text"—the dominant manuscript tradition at the time—and published in 1516. New manuscript discoveries have led to minor adjustments to that text, and where uncertainty remains about exact wording or authenticity, the margins of honest modern versions will tell us so. The New King James, for instance, while still following the received text, notes these things conscientiously as it goes along.

Other things being equal, manuscripts are "better" when they are nearer to the original—that is, earlier in date.

In the New Testament only one word per one thousand is in any way doubtful, and no point of doctrine is lost when verses not "in better manuscripts" are omitted. (As examples, see Matt. 6:13b, 17:21, 18:11; Mark 9:44, 46, 49, 16:9–20; Luke 23:17; John 5:4; and Acts 8:37.) Such has been God's "singular care and providence" in preserving his written Word for us (Westminster Confession I.viii).

So how does all this bear on the Christian's very proper faith in biblical inerrancy—that is, the total truth and trustworthiness of the true text and all it teaches?

Holy Scripture is, according to the view of Jesus and his apostles, God preaching, instructing, showing, and telling us things, and testifying to himself through the human witness of prophets, poets, theological narrators of history, and philosophical observers of life. The Bible's inerrancy is not the inerrancy of any one published text or version, nor of anyone's interpretation, nor of any scribal slips or pious inauthentic additions acquired during transmission.

Rather, scriptural inerrancy relates to the human writer's expressed meaning in each book, and to the Bible's whole body of revealed truth and wisdom.

Belief in inerrancy involves an advance commitment to receive as from God all that the Bible, interpreting itself to us through the Holy Spirit in a natural and coherent way, teaches. Thus it shapes our understanding of biblical authority.

So inerrantists should welcome the work of textual scholars, who are forever trying to eliminate the inauthentic and give us exactly what the biblical writers wrote, neither more nor less. The way into God's mind is through his penmen's minds, precisely as expressed, under his guidance, in their own words as they wrote them.

Text criticism serves inerrancy; they are friends. Inerrancy treasures the meaning of each writer's words, while text criticism checks that we have each writer's words pure and intact. Both these wisdoms are needed if we are to benefit fully from the written Word of God.

J. I. Packer is a senior editor of Christianity Today *and is the Board of Governors' Professor of Theology at Regent College in Vancouver. He is the author of multiple books, including his seminal work* Knowing God. *"Text Criticism and Inerrancy" was first published in* Christianity Today, *October 7, 2002. Vol. 46, No. 11, Page 102.*

Open Up

Select one of these activities to launch your discussion time.

Option 1

Discuss these icebreaker questions:

- What are some adjectives that come to mind for you as important ways to describe the Bible?
- Have you ever tried to answer an unbeliever's skepticism about the Bible's trustworthiness? What happened?
- Have you ever struggled with doubt about the Scriptures? Explain.

Option 2

Play a tougher version of the children's game "Telephone." Begin by privately writing down a two- to four-sentence light-hearted fictional story about someone in your group that includes several specific details. For example, *Rob went out for dessert last night and got a double-scoop sundae with Chunky Monkey and Rocky Road. The whole thing was topped with cherries, hot fudge, and whipped cream . . . and a Japanese beetle who landed on top when Rob wasn't looking. Crunch!*

Once everyone's written a short story, form a line. Whoever is at the head of the line should whisper his or her written story in the ear of the person next in line. He or she should then do their best to whisper it word-for-word to the next person, and so on. Once the story makes it to the end of the line, the last person should recite the story aloud, word for word.

The person at the head of the line then reads the real story—you all can laugh about how similar or dissimilar the starting and ending stories are.

After you've played several rounds of the game, talk about these questions:

- How does this game compare or contrast with the way the text of the Bible has been passed along to modern readers today?
- Which challenges in this game might relate to the challenges of transmitting Scripture across cultures and centuries? And how does it differ?

■ The Issue

It is not unusual to have questions about the Bible's reliability. Not only do non-Christians doubt it; sometimes we Christians do as well. Common doubts about the biblical text include:

- *It's so old—it must have changed over time.*
- *Original copies of the manuscripts don't even exist anymore. Anyone could have made it up.*
- *If we knew what the original texts really said, we wouldn't need so many different translations.*

The Bible invites these kinds of arguments because it makes such outrageous claims—that it contains the words of Almighty God, that it is absolutely true and trustworthy, and that it is the foundation for all Christian beliefs. Fortunately for us, the Bible also has some incredibly powerful defenders: generations of faithful scribes, an army of textual scholars, and God himself.

- Discuss the meaning of the words *inerrant, reliable, authoritative,* and *trustworthy* when it comes to reading Scripture. Are some words more helpful to you than others? Why or why not?

- Why do you trust Scripture? How has it proved true and trustworthy in your life? Share an example from your life that's meaningful to you.

Reflect

Take a moment to read Deuteronomy 4:1–14; John 8:12–26; 2 Timothy 3:14–17; and Hebrews 1:1–2 on your own. Record your observations: Which phrases or words jump out at you? What are the key ideas in these texts? How do these texts inform your understanding of the Bible's trustworthiness?

Let's Explore

The Bible was compiled with great discernment.

As Packer reminds us, Bible manuscripts were hand-copied from ancient times through the Middle Ages. This might sound like the textual equivalent of the party game "Telephone," but these copyists, called scribes, were professionals, and they took their job extremely seriously.

Jewish scribes, who kept up the Old Testament scrolls for centuries, had a nearly foolproof system for making perfect copies. First, a scribe would count the number of letters on the page to be copied. When he had finished his copy, he would count the number of letters on the new page and make sure it matched the original. Two or three other scribes would then check the copied page.

Christian scribes also took great pains in creating and proofing their pages. The gorgeous lettering and elaborate artwork in many medieval Bibles attest to hours of intense effort.

Most scholars are amazed at how well the scribes' system worked. With the momentous discovery of the Dead Sea Scrolls in the 1940s and '50s, some people looked forward to exposing discrepancies between the ancient Dead Sea manuscripts and the more familiar later texts. In fact, while the Dead Sea Scrolls have prompted a few shifts in biblical scholarship, they mainly served to affirm that Christians already had excellent texts.

Though inconsistencies in the biblical texts are rare, there are some portions of Scripture that are somewhat problematic. Look together at two larger sections of Scripture included in most Bibles that have questionable reliability: Mark 16:9–20 and John 7:53–8:11. Be sure to read the notes preceding the text or as footnotes in your Bible.

- Were you aware that these segments of Scripture are not found in the earliest manuscripts? What's your reaction to this—do you find it unsettling or problematic? If so, why? If not, explain your reaction.

- Which stands out to you? Do these examples or notes like those in Mark 16:9–20 or John 7:53–8:11 affect your "trust" in the Bible? Why or why not?

At its best, textual scholarship refines written works by comparing different versions to determine the most reliable manuscripts, giving special weight to older versions and versions of which more copies exist. At its worst, textual scholarship undermines written works by attacking them with radical skepticism and biased agendas. Sadly, some people have used such bad scholarship to suggest that the Bible is totally unreliable or that obscure texts, particularly those that support unorthodox beliefs, are better than standard texts.

The average Christian will never know enough about textual scholarship to sort all of this out. That's okay, though, because specialists have been on the job for centuries—and it hasn't been easy.

Read 2 Timothy 3:14–17.

This is a classic text on the soundness of the Bible. It's important to note, though, that at the time Paul wrote these words to Timothy, "all Scripture" (verse 16) only included the Old Testament. Paul probably had no idea that his letters would someday be called Scripture. Most of the rest of the New Testament, including the Gospels, hadn't even been written yet.

Within decades of Paul's letter, dozens if not hundreds of Christian and pseudo-Christian manuscripts were circulating throughout the Near East. Disagreements over which manuscripts were the best prompted church leaders to begin ranking them, prizing those written closest to the time of Jesus, those written by people with direct connections to Jesus, and those that stayed truest to the teachings of Jesus. In 367 Bishop Athanasius of Alexandria wrote an official letter listing the twenty-seven books that he and other church authorities believed should become the Christian Scriptures. Those twenty-seven books became the New Testament we still use today.

The next big moment in Bible text history came a few years later with the efforts of a scholar named Jerome. Lots of Latin translations of Scripture were floating around in his day, not all of them good. Jerome was asked to create a standard version so all Christian churches could, literally, be reading from the same page. He nailed down the New Testament, working from well-known Greek manuscripts, then took the extra step of learning Hebrew to do the Old Testament. (Latin scholars before him usually worked from Greek translations of the Hebrew, meaning they got all of their texts secondhand.)

Jerome's translation, the Vulgate (meaning "common"), remained the standard for more than one thousand years. Great as it was, though, it wasn't perfect. During the Renaissance, when many ancient manuscripts were rediscovered in the West, scholars like Erasmus (c. 1469–1536) went back to the originals and improved on Jerome's work.

A flurry of Bibles in common European languages followed. Some, like the King James Version, were based mostly on Jerome's work. Others, like William Tyndale's Bible, were based on fresh reading of the original texts. Debates over the different versions grew bitter, but there is no question that all of this work brought Christians closer to understanding what the biblical writers actually wrote and what they meant by it.

- What does it mean to you that Scripture is "inspired by God" (2 Timothy 3:14–17)? How has Scripture made you wise or equipped you? Share a recent example.

- In light of what you've read and discussed so far about the history of Scripture's compilation, translation, and transmission, how would you explain the trustworthiness of Scripture to a non-Christian? Or how would you communicate it to a new Christian?

God desires to communicate with us.

Read Deuteronomy 4:1–14.

It is clear that God took great effort to connect with this special community. Rather than uttering indecipherable noises or symbols, God chose to create words that were part of everyday communication, even inscribing these instructions into a permanent record, as in the Ten Commandments.

The important point, as Moses says in Deuteronomy 4, is that God initiated the covenant and therefore sought from the beginning to communicate in a truthful and authoritative manner to the people he had chosen. The Bible is not an arbitrary collection of cute, nice, or even wise writings that simply amassed themselves together in some dusty corner of a Jewish rabbi's personal library; it is a set of literary creations built on the foundation of God speaking words of covenant relationship to Israel through Moses.

- How does the idea of a covenant document created at Mount Sinai connect with your understanding of the Bible and its purposes?

God not only spoke to the Israelites, he also speaks to us today. Read Hebrews 1:1–2.

- What does it mean to you that God is not silent or distant, but that he *speaks* to us through Christ and through Scripture? How would your life be different if you didn't believe in a God who speaks to us?

- How have you encountered God or heard from him through his Word recently? How has the Holy Spirit convicted you or given you guidance through Scripture? Share a specific example of a verse or passage through which God has communicated with you.

God is truthful, thus his word is reliable.

Read John 8:12–26.

- What was Jesus seeking to communicate to those who dialogued with him in John 8?

- Why does Jesus make such a strong contrast between the truth and the lie? How does this inform us about the truthfulness of the Bible?

When Jesus was challenged by those around him to declare more fully his identity, he simply said that he was from God and that God was faithful. In the lengthy dialogue of John 8, Jesus asserted that our human tendency is to twist facts, fudge on truth, and even tell outright lies. But God, Jesus reminded us, is always truthful, reliable, and "light" over the darkness of deception. In fact, truth derives its character from God.

Jesus also tied God directly to Old Testament Scripture in this passage. It is the reliable truthfulness of God, which spoke through the "Law and the Prophets," and thus provided the background and testimony as to who Jesus is. This helps us draw out the long line of continuity in Scripture. If the Old Testament was begun as covenant documents in Exodus 20–24 and accumulated related writings, which further fleshed out the meaning and impact of this covenant, Jesus comes now in New Testament times as the fulfillment of the Old Covenant promises and expectations.

This is a primary element of biblical faith. God is truthful, and the Bible is an extension of that divine reliability. Furthermore, Jesus both witnesses to that truth and embodies it. He is, as he claimed to his disciples at the Last Supper, the expression of the New Covenant, which fulfills and augments the Old Covenant that shaped Israel's existence from the time of Mount Sinai forward.

Going Forward

Discuss this question as a group:

- Do you think believing the Bible's trustworthiness requires a leap of faith? Or can such a belief be based on inquiry, evidence, and rational conclusions? Explain.

Read the following aloud together, then discuss the final questions:

If the Bible were any other text, the testimony of the faithful scribes and textual scholars would be enough to prove its authenticity. But the stakes are immeasurably high for the Bible, because Christians set their life by it. People may still wonder, *Athanasius sounds like a great guy, but how can we be sure he picked the right books for the New Testament? What if there are other books, or older manuscripts, or passages that translators are totally wrong about?*

Let's remember that Athanasius didn't make an arbitrary decision. The books he listed were already commonly used throughout the church, not in the order he listed them, and not consistently, but there already was broad consensus on which books were inspired by God for the church's use. Athanasius merely solidified a movement that had been developing for three hundred years. The church recognized the books and letters that the Holy Spirit was using to change lives for Christ.

Ultimately, of course, the responsibility for the Bible lies with God. Only he knows his message perfectly and can make perfectly sure that his people receive it. Christians must take this on faith.

- How can a person acknowledge minor grammatical errors or rare variances in the original manuscripts and translations of the Bible and still claim the Bible to be infallible, inerrant, and completely trustworthy? How would you explain this point of view to a skeptic?

- How do you desire to grow in your trust in and reliance upon God's Word in your life?

Pray together by reading aloud Psalm 119:9–16, emphasizing each statement about God's Word.

Do we really need so many Bible translations . . . and do we need one more?

SCRIPTURE FOCUS

- Deuteronomy 8:1–3
- Psalm 23:1–2
- John 1:14–18
- 1 Peter 1:23–25

SESSION 3

LOST IN TRANSLATION?

How many translations of the Bible are there? How many do we need? Apparently, at least one more, according to Raymond C. Van Leeuwen. The most popular versions of the Bible are influenced by a type of translation called "functional equivalence," the effort to make the text understandable to modern hearers. But Van Leeuwen says something is getting lost in the translation. In this study, we'll examine some of the textual issues he raises in his *Christianity Today* article "We Really Do Need Another Bible Translation." We'll search out what's changing and unchanging about the eternal Word of God.

Before You Meet

Read "We Really Do Need Another Bible Translation" from *Christianity Today*.

WE REALLY DO NEED ANOTHER BIBLE TRANSLATION

As good as many modern versions are, they often do not allow us to hear what the Holy Spirit actually said.

by Raymond C. Van Leeuwen

Translations are both a gift and a problem for the body of Christ. As members of that body, we are called to think and live biblically. Especially since the Reformation called the church to *biblical* renewal, we have been afforded many Bible translations that have shaped the language, thought, and life of the West.

More recently, a wealth of new translations has enabled millions to read the Bible in language that is not forbiddingly difficult or foreign to them. All this was and remains a great gift to the church. I myself am honored to have made a small contribution to the New Living Translation (NLT).

But translation is also a problem. Every translation imperfectly represents the original, because languages and cultures differ in ways that translation by itself cannot overcome. Translations interpose a fallible human interpretation between us and the infallible Word. These basic problems affect all translations. But the increase in Bible translations during the last sixty years has created new problems for the church.

Newer translations—the NLT, New International Version (NIV), New Revised Standard Version (NRSV), Revised English Bible (REB; a revision of the New English Bible), and Today's English Version (TEV, also called The Good News Bible), among others—are all influenced by a theory called dynamic or "functional equivalence" (FE) translation. Such translations serve their intended purposes and audiences well. More important, they have led many to Christ. But I and a growing number of linguist-translators believe FE theory is inadequate as the only model for translation. (Translations themselves are often better and sometimes worse than their theories.) Linguists argue that the church needs not one but several types of translation, each with its own use. That's why I'm advocating another modern translation, one that works from a different theory than FE.

How Did We Get to this Point?

FE theory is closely identified with an evangelical who, over the last half century, has done more to foster Bible translation around the world than anyone else. His name is Eugene Nida, and every translator today has been affected by his work. Even secular translators pay homage to Nida. His theory and practice of translation was first called "dynamic equivalence" translation and, later, "functional equivalence" translation. If you read a Bible translated in the last half-century, you probably read a Bible influenced by Nida.

In the 1940s, Nida and others of the American Bible Society developed practical guidelines for missionary translators working among peoples who often did not have a written language, let alone a Bible, to read. Bible translators learned that they had to make translations understandable to people with little access to preachers and teachers, and whose culture was different from the world of King David or of Jesus and the apostles. They made translations that often supplied the information needed by isolated tribal peoples. In doing so, they often changed what the original said, somewhat like an explanatory paraphrase.

It is this type of translation (focusing on ease of understanding for the intended reader) that has become dominant, not only in the Two-Thirds World but also in the modern West, with its long history of Bible teaching and preaching and its seminaries and colleges, to train leaders in Scripture and biblical languages.

Parallel events took place in the English-speaking world. In the twentieth century, older English translations seemed increasingly out of date and difficult to read, especially for new Christians. Many became discouraged and gave up reading the Bible for themselves. Practically speaking, many Christians lost the Bible with its "power to save" and to give wisdom for right living here and now (see Rom. 1:16 and 2 Tim. 3:15–17). They also were in danger of losing touch with Christ himself; without the Bible, we do not have Christ in his fullness, for it alone shows us who Jesus is infallibly.

As society changed and the Bible seemed increasingly foreign, a variety of attempts were made to make the Book more accessible.

In the 1940s, J. B. Phillips began producing his New Testament "in modern English," as the title eventually proclaimed. He followed an already established British tradition of offering expansive, interpretive readings of Scripture that tried to lay out in easily understandable language what was said more briefly and pregnantly in Scripture. Phillips's work got many people reading the Bible again, in paraphrase form. In America, the director of Moody Press, Kenneth Taylor, realized that his children were not understanding the Bible as it was devoutly read at the family dinner table. So, on his daily train ride to work, he began to rewrite the family King James Version in language that his kids could understand and enjoy. It turned out that The Living Bible (its eventual name) not only helped the Taylor children but fulfilled the desire of millions of Americans for a Bible that was not difficult, a Bible that made sense to them.

Phillips and Taylor both retold the Bible in familiar, explanatory language—a procedure FE translations imitate. Phillips worked from the original languages; Taylor did not. But they helped pave the way for FE translations.

A Christian missionary translator and linguist, Ernst-August Gutt, believes that there can be several types of translation (one of which is FE), depending on the purpose and audience of the translation. What is crucial is that readers are made aware of what type of translation they are dealing with. A paraphrase or story Bible is not a translation, though it is useful for many readers.

FE translations (again, most Bibles today) often change the language, images, and metaphors of Scripture to make understanding easier. But for serious study, readers need a translation that is more transparent to the "otherness" of Scripture. We need a translation that allows the Bible to say what it says, even if that seems strange and odd to readers at first glance. If God is "other" than we are, we should be willing to work at the "otherness" of the Bible in order to understand what the Lord is saying through his Word. The purpose of the Bible is not to make Jesus like us, but to make us like Christ. The Bible is designed to change us, to make us different, heirs of Abraham according to the promise fulfilled in Christ (Acts 2).

We need translations for people who are eager and willing to make the effort to overcome the difficulty of reading a book that is in fact foreign to us. Indeed, when we come to serious Bible study, whether in a church group, Sunday school, or college classroom, this type of translation becomes necessary, for we are trying to get as close as possible within the limits of our own language. When the martyr and translator William Tyndale did this, he shaped the English language in ways that were biblical. The KJV translators who inherited Tyndale's work gave the English-speaking world a Bible that shaped its language, life, and faith for hundreds of years. The danger of FE translations is that they shape the Bible too much to fit our world and our expectations. There is a danger that the Bible gets silenced because we have tamed and domesticated it.

Troubles in Translation

It is hard to know what the Bible *means* when we are uncertain about what it *says*. In class, teachers with Greek and Hebrew often find themselves retranslating a passage to show students more directly what the literal Hebrew or Greek said.

The problem with FE translations (i.e., most modern translations) is that they prevent the reader from inferring biblical *meaning* because they change what the Bible *said*.

Comparing a few translated verses with those of the KJV, the classic, more direct translation will illustrate my point. The KJV translates part of Colossians 3:9–10 as "Ye have put off the old man with his deeds; and have put on the new *man*." The KJV at this point offers a transparent or direct translation of the Greek. (I prefer not to call it "literal" because translations always add, change, and subtract from the original. The only literal Bible is written in Hebrew and Greek.)

A transparent translation conveys as much as possible of what was said and how it was said, in as near word-for-word form as the target language allows, though inevitably with some difference and imperfectly.

In this verse, the KJV translators even alert readers, with the use of italics, that the second instance of the word *man* is not actually in the Greek text, though it's pretty clear that it is meant by the original. (Just as we might say to a waitress, "My daughter will have fries, and I will [have fries] too"—we leave out the phrase in brackets because it is clearly understood.)

"The old man . . . the new *man*"—the English words are simple and clear, like the Greek. What Paul *said* here is plain. What he *meant* is not, at least to most readers. For Paul, all humans are included "in Adam" or "in Christ," and at present, Christians live an uneasy existence in both camps. In Colossians 3, "the old man" refers to *Adam*, the first man (Gen. 1–5), and "the new *man*" refers to *Christ*, the last Adam and true "image of God" (Col. 1:15; Rom. 5:12–21; 1 Cor. 15:45–50; Eph. 4:22–24).

Jesus makes right and restores all that the first man corrupted. In Christ the purposes of God for creation and "man" are fulfilled. So when Paul says "put on the new man," he means "put on the Lord Jesus Christ," as he says in Romans 13:14 (see Gal. 3:27). Today it might be better to translate the phrases as "the old Adam . . . . the new Adam," to show that Paul preaches Christ in Old Testament terms. In Genesis, Paul's Greek Old Testament (the Septuagint) translated "Adam" as *ho anthropos*, "the man," and since the Septuagint was the version all Gentile churches used, the reference to Adam would be picked up at once.

Paul's literal *words* here are easy to understand, but his *meaning* requires more effort. The meaning of Paul's words depends upon background knowledge and context not found in Colossians 3. Some of the necessary background is given in the preceding paragraph. The issue of context is more complex.

Paul wrote two thousand years ago in a different context. Can his words be relevant in our context today? Yes. Though humans live in many different situations, all Christians through time and space relate to Christ in the same way that Paul's first readers did. Their lives and ours are "hidden in Christ" (Col. 3:3). Our ultimate, common context is Christ, "in whom all things were created . . . in whom all things hold together" (Col. 1:16–17)—though our particular contexts may differ.

There are several ways readers can quickly gain the outside knowledge they need to infer the meaning of Paul's words. Pastors and teachers with a knowledge of Greek can help them. Study Bibles and commentaries can help. Reading and rereading the entire Bible in a direct translation is best of all, though it is slower and harder.

Newer FE translations, however, try to short-circuit the problem of background and context by changing what was written. They do not so much translate Paul's *words* into English words as try to find a *meaning* already familiar to Americans. They hope the new American meaning will affect readers the same way Paul's meaning affected his readers. The two meanings are meant to be functionally equivalent.

Let us see if newer FE type translations succeed in their goal at Colossians 3:9–10. Here are two attempts:

1. "You have taken off *your old self* with its practices and have put on the new self" (NIV; compare NRSV, TEV).
2. "You have discarded *the old human nature* and the conduct that goes with it, and have put on *the new nature* which is constantly being renewed" (REB; compare RSV).

Most Americans have ideas about their (inner and outer) self and its renewal and can talk about it in all sorts of words and ways. We get a new religion or hairdo and say, "Look at the new me!" We build our biceps or ego and talk about our "new self-image." We have various ideas about human nature too; perhaps that it is sinful or basically good. But are our modern meanings the same as Paul's? Do translations 1 and 2 really help us understand what Paul said and meant?

I think not. Translations like "your old self" and "new self" may unwittingly lead readers away from Christ ("the new *man*") to the individual *self*, one of America's greatest idols. And while Paul's "man" refers concretely and specifically to Adam and Christ, "human nature" is an abstract, philosophical idea whose meaning changes with the wind. Both translations prevent readers from learning that the "new man" is not us but Christ.

We become new persons only "in Christ" (Gal. 3:27) and by taking off Adam and putting on Christ, who is our *life* (Col. 3:3). By seeking familiar modern meanings, these newer translations make it much harder to see the deep biblical pattern of Paul's thought. They obscure the words and metaphors by which the Spirit has woven a coherent tapestry of meaning that stretches from Genesis to Revelation. This practice removes the information we need to understand, because it hides the Bible's dynamic unity and coherence.

Biblical metaphors drop into our hearts like a seed in soil and make us think, precisely because they are not obvious at first. The translator who removes biblical metaphors to make the text "easier" for readers may defeat the purpose of the Holy Spirit, who chose a metaphor in the first place. Metaphors grab us and work on us and in us. They have the spiritual power to transform our minds. The abandonment of basic biblical metaphors in many translations follows naturally from FE theory, because the target languages may not use such expressions. But it is the foreignness of metaphors that is their virtue. Metaphors make us stop and think, *Now what does* that *mean?*

It is not clear to me that replacing metaphors with abstractions makes it easier for readers. "God is my rock" is just as easy to understand as "God is my firm support" but means far more. "Walk in love" is simple, as is FE's "live a life of love" (Eph. 5:2, NIV). But "walk in love" resonates with the rich system of biblical metaphor rooted in Old Testament wisdom, where life is journey on a good or bad way, and in Acts, where Christianity became known as "the Way" (Acts 9:2). Metaphors are multifaceted and function to invoke active thought on the part of the receiver. Receivers must think and feel their way through a metaphor, and it is this very process that gives the metaphor its power to take hold of receivers as they take hold of it.

Similar problems occur in Hebrews 2:5–9, when the NRSV changes RSV's direct translation "son of man" to "mortals" (plural), thus obscuring the crucial link between "son of man" in Psalm 8:4–8 and Jesus. This NRSV change from direct to FE translation also destroys the link with Jesus as the "son of man" in the Gospels prefigured in Daniel 7.

Here are some other examples of FE translations' obscuring the text.

A. In Galatians 5:16–26, Paul contrasts "the works of the flesh" with "the fruit of the Spirit" (RSV, NRSV). Paul's words here and elsewhere have often been misunderstood as meaning an opposition between the Spirit and our unspiritual "material" body. To avoid this misunderstanding, the New Jerusalem Bible (NJB) renders "flesh" as "self-indulgence," while the NIV speaks of "sinful nature" (with a footnote on *flesh*). This does two things: it prevents us from finding out why Paul used the Greek word for "flesh," and it may mislead us to infer that human nature is sinful or evil, even though the "Word became flesh" (John 1:14).

B. In Ecclesiastes (and only in Ecclesiastes), the NIV translates *hebel* as "meaningless." *Hebel* is the most important word in Ecclesiastes and appears thirty-seven times; its translation dramatically shapes our understanding of the entire book. *Hebel* means something like "breath," "mist," or "fog" (See James 4:14, "What is your life? A mist"). In Ecclesiastes *hebel* describes life metaphorically, as a breath, mist, or fog. Unfortunately, the NIV's interpretation forces readers to read the book only one way, and to conclude roughly that life without God is meaningless. Other scholars are convinced that Ecclesiastes does *not* say life is "meaningless" but that it is like a breath or fog—hard to grasp, beyond control, sometimes impenetrable, here today and gone tomorrow.

My point is not primarily whether the NIV is right or wrong but that its abstract interpretation denies the church access to what the Spirit *actually said*. (In this respect, the KJV translators also missed the mark by choosing vanity.) Translation may too quickly interpose interpretation that interferes with the priestly and prophetic calling of believers. "Meaningless" also makes Ecclesiastes seem a "foreign body" in the Bible, instead of a book whose reflections on life as God's gift and as "breath" have much in common with the Psalms (144:3–4), Job (7:7, 16–18), Isaiah (40:6–8, using a different metaphor), Jesus (Matt. 6:25–34), and James.

When our translations do not say what the Hebrew or Greek say, it is hard to know what the Bible means. We need to understand better why these problems arise. A look at the translator's task will help us.

1 2 3 4 5 6 7 8

What Translators Do

At their best, Bible translations richly convey what God has said and can enrich the understanding of even those who read the original languages. Yet translation is a difficult and, in some ways, impossible task. Translations always compromise and interpret.

Depending on context, the same words can mean different things. "Money talks" means one thing as a boast made by the man who bribed the jury, another when spoken by the innocent victim. "Yeah, yeah" may mean "Yes, yes!" Spoken with a cynical voice, it means "Blah, blah, I don't believe you." Listeners and readers necessarily infer the meaning of what was said or, in stories, what happened. Much of our ability to understand language depends on knowledge not found in the words themselves.

Take another example. Suppose, just before bedtime, an insomniac is asked, "Would you like some coffee?" She responds simply, "Coffee would keep me awake." Her host correctly infers something like "No thank you, I do not want coffee now"—even though this was never said. But suppose coffee is offered to Homer Simpson struggling to stay awake at the nuclear power plant. When Homer says the very same words ("Coffee would keep me awake"), we know he means "Yes! Yes! Bring me coffee!" (and probably "Don't forget the donuts!" as well). In each case, there is a gap between *what was said* and *what was meant* in a particular context. This gap can be bridged only by inference based on unspoken background knowledge and context.

There may also be a gap between *what was said and meant* and *what is inferred.* These gaps may or may not be bridged successfully. Sometimes we get it wrong. Here I offer my own perception of what is involved in translation and understanding.

A translator's first and most important job is to bridge the language gap. She seeks the best way of saying in English what was said first in Hebrew or Greek. But even this is not simple. No English word fully matches a Greek or Hebrew word. For instance, the biblical words for "soul" are the Hebrew *nephesh* and the Greek *psyche.* Unfortunately, *nephesh* is also translated as "life," "appetite," "neck," and "person," among other words. We may think that only humans "have souls," that "souls are immortal" and that Jesus "saves souls."

But in Hebrew, both man and beast are "living *nephesh*," and a dead person is a "dead *nephesh*." In biblical Hebrew and Greek, to save a *nephesh* or *psyche* means to save a life or person. The shed, sacrificial blood of Jesus atones for our "lives" according to the law of Leviticus, because "the life (*nephesh*) is in the blood" (Lev. 17:11–14). Even the best translator is forced to choose English words, none of which exactly matches the Hebrew or Greek.

The matter is not trivial. Biblical salvation restores the whole creation. To "save souls" in the sense of saving a "spiritual" part of us is not biblical. The New Testament teaches the resurrection of the body, and life in a new creation where heaven comes down to earth. As our earlier biblical examples showed, even when a translation captures what was said in clear, simple English, we may not understand what it means or its relevance today. "Put on the new man" is clear English, but few realize Paul means Christ. We lack the background biblical knowledge and extended context for us to correctly infer what he meant by what he said.

Reading the Whole Bible

For us moderns to understand the Bible, we have to learn a lot about the world of the Bible and the world in the Bible; otherwise it just doesn't make sense. For example, Leviticus is an entire book designed to teach us what holiness is—something we Christians desperately need: "Just as he who called you is holy, so be holy in all you do; for it is written, 'Be holy, because I am holy'" (1 Pet. 1:15–16, quoting Lev. 11:44–45).

Without knowing the meaning of *holy, clean*, and *unclean*, and of *blood* and *leprosy* in the Book of Leviticus, we do not fully understand the story of Samson, the lion, and the honey. Nor do we fully see the point of Jesus's healing lepers and the woman with an issue of blood. Holiness is much more than "separation"—though that is part of it. It means freedom from that "uncleanness" that puts us out of joint with God and man. Holiness means harmony with God, ourselves, our neighbors, and the creation (see Gordon Wenham's very helpful *The Book of Leviticus* [Eerdmans, 1979]).

Salvation is to make us holy so that God can dwell among his people (Exod. 29:45–46; Rev. 21:3), and we can be as he is: holy (Lev. 19:2; 1 Pet. 1:15–16). Indeed, at the end of Exodus, the descent of God to fill the "house" with his glory is the Old Testament Pentecost (Exod. 40:34–38). And after this Old Testament Pentecost, Nadab and Abihu are the Old Testament precursors of Ananias and Sapphira (Lev. 10:1–11; Acts 5:1–11). Both pairs offend God's holy presence as he makes a crucial new beginning in the history of redemption.

A Translation We Need Today

My concern has been that the dominance of FE translations has made it more difficult for English readers to know what the Bible actually said. We need an up-to-date translation that is more transparent to the original languages. If the translator's task is to negotiate the difficult balance between faithfulness to the original text and offering immediate sense in the target language, a direct translation will lean toward the original text.

As a member of Christ's body and a Bible teacher, I am pleading for a type of translation that is more consistently transparent, so that the original shines through it to the extent permitted by the target language.

A direct translator will, in a learned and aesthetically appropriate way, use the resources of the target language to richly capture the details of the original, even though readers may be challenged by some of the Bible's foreignness. The Bible creates a vast context of meaning through cross-references and allusions, phrases and metaphors, echoes and types. For readers to discover this type of biblical meaning in their translations, translators of the Bible must be constantly aware of parallel passages, expressions, and images. Where this does not happen, much of the text's actual meaning may be lost, often to be replaced by modern meanings.

Adam and Eve fell when they became uncertain about God's Word to them in the Garden. They heard a word from the snake about how to live, a word that contradicted God's Word. Eve decided to decide for herself which word to follow. Like Israel, we and our children live in a polytheistic society where many "gods" offer competing words, each claiming to show the way, the truth, and the life. Mammon and Baal, money and sex, self and greed shout loudly. The church needs linguists and translators, preachers and teachers, scholars and laity who will help us all hear God's Word clearly and live it rightly, until he comes again.

Raymond C. Van Leeuwen is professor of Biblical Studies at Eastern College in St. Davids, Pennsylvania. He is indebted to Dr. Barrie Evans of Kent, England, for his long-standing help in linguistics. A more extensive treatment of this topic appears in the book After Pentecost *(Zondervan). "We Really Do Need Another Bible Translation" was first published in* Christianity Today, *October 22, 2001; Vol. 45, No. 13, Page 28.*

■ Open Up

Select one of these activities to launch your discussion time.

Option 1

Discuss these icebreaker questions:

- Have you ever had a funny or challenging experience trying to communicate in another language? Describe it.
- Have you ever had difficulty understanding a different dialect of English (such as British English, Southern v. Northern accent, urban lingo, and so on)? Share a personal experience with the group and brainstorm together some differences in dialect within the English language.

Option 2

Form pairs and try your hand at "translating" the text below into contemporary English. Select at least one pair to do a *direct translation* (word by word) rendering it in more modern language. All the remaining pairs should seek to translate using *functional equivalence* (identifying the key concepts and then seeking to communicate those concepts in modern terms). Translate your text as quickly as possible—in five minutes or less!

Text: The Prologue of William Shakespeare's *Romeo and Juliet*

Two households, both alike in dignity,
In fair Verona, where we lay our scene,
From ancient grudge break to new mutiny,
Where civil blood makes civil hands unclean.
From forth the fatal loins of these two foes
A pair of star-cross'd lovers take their life;
Whole misadventured piteous overthrows
Do with their death bury their parents' strife.
The fearful passage of their death-mark'd love,
And the continuance of their parents' rage,
Which, but their children's end, nought could remove,
Is now the two hours' traffic of our stage;
The which if you with patient ears attend,
What here shall miss, our toil shall strive to mend.

When five minutes are up, read the texts to each other (even if they aren't finished), then vote to select the best one!

Talk about these questions together:

- Which do you prefer? Shakespeare's English or the modern Americanized versions? Why?
- What is gained and what is lost by "translating" this text into modern language?

The Issue

- Which translation of the Bible is your favorite? Why?

- Take a moment to discuss your general impressions of the various English Bible translations you know of, such as the New International Version, the King James Version, the New Century Version, or the New Living Translation.

  For example . . .

  _____Which translation would you choose if you were purchasing a Bible for a spiritual seeker who wanted to check out Christianity?
  _____Which translation is good for new Christians?
  _____Which one would you recommend for children? for teens?
  _____Which version is best for personal devotions?
  _____Which translation is good for in-depth Bible study?

Almost everyone has a favorite translation of Scripture. But Van Leeuwen says all modern translations have been affected by attempts to make the Bible more easily understood by modern readers, and not all of these effects are good. Some of the hard-to-grasp truths of Scripture should remain hard to grasp.

■ Reflect

Take a moment to read Deuteronomy 8:1–3; Psalm 23:1–2; John 1:14–18; and 1 Peter 1:23–25. Record your observations, making note of the key points and ideas communicated in each passage. Read some of the passages in more than one Bible translation. (If you only have one translation at home, you can look up the verses online in multiple versions at www.biblegateway.com.)

■ Let's Explore

The value of biblical language is in its time-bound nature.

Sometimes the language of Scripture is foreign. The language of the Bible captures times and places far removed from our twenty-first century society. That is part of its beauty. That is also a reason that readers of the

Bible should be educated about the language of Scripture and the culture it represents.

Obscure meanings have always forced us to study language more carefully. Luke, who wrote his Gospel especially for Gentile readers, frequently included interpretations of Jewish customs for people with different religious and social backgrounds. In this way, he preserved the rich meaning of the Jewish heritage for non-Jewish readers.

Sometimes the language of Scripture is earthy. The Greeks had developed words for philosophical concepts, which were especially useful in the New Testament. The Hebrews, however, had a language of fewer words rooted in ordinary life. For example, Van Leeuwen points out that the NIV renders the word *mist* in Ecclesiastes as "meaningless" and the NCV as "useless." In the original text, an abstract concept is compared to an ordinary early morning fog.

Consider also the author's references to *nephesh* and *psyche*. The Hebrew word *nephesh* means "soul." But it can also mean "neck," "appetite," "person," or "life." By choosing to render the word as "soul," the translator limits our understanding of the word. That also jeopardizes our interpretation of the text in relation to other passages. When Paul refers to *psyche*, he speaks of the soul as a part of the person apart from the body. But when Hebrew writers speak of the whole person, they use the word *nephesh*. In these contexts, both words are translated as "soul," and the difference between them often eludes the reader. Contemporary readers only see this difference when they dig into the text with several translations, or, better yet, use study tools that reveal multiple usages of the original languages.

Read Psalm 23:1–2.

- Are there other effective ways you can think of to translate "the Lord is my shepherd" or "I am the good Shepherd"?

The value of biblical language is in its eternal nature.

The following is John 1:14–18 as rendered in *The New Greek-English Interlinear New Testament* (Tyndale, 1990). This is an attempt to render the Greek text into English as literally as possible. You can see that word-for-word translation is not possible, because some Hebrew and Greek words require more than one English word in translation or because they have no English equivalent. Notice too that the syntax, or the order of words in sentences, is different.

Read this passage aloud:

> 14 And the word flesh became and tabernacled among us, and we gazed [upon] the glory of him, glory as of an only one from [the] father, full of grace and truth.
> 15 John testifies about him and has cried out saying, This one was he [as to] whom I said, the one after me coming before me has become, because prior to me he was.
> 16 Because from the fullness of him we all received even grace on top grace.
> 17 Because the law through Moses was given, the grace and the truth through Jesus Christ came.
> 18 God no one has seen ever; an only one, God, the one being in the bosom of the father, that one explained [him].

Now take turns trying to render or paraphrase each verse in everyday English. Next, read John 1:14–18 aloud from one of your Bibles.

- What's your reaction to this "direct" translation? What do we gain in the attempt to translate directly? What do we lose?

- Linguists frequently remind us that "all translation is interpretation." How is this statement borne out in the exercise you just did?

Read 1 Peter 1:23–25, where Peter quotes Isaiah.

- How does the Word of God transcend time and culture? What does it mean that the Word of God lives forever? Explain the truth of this passage in your own words.

When translating Scripture for specific people groups, particularly those who may have no written version of the Bible, translators face a difficult challenge: how best to communicate eternal truths in language and concepts the audience will understand. Should cultural "equivalents" be used? Or should a more direct translation be employed? For example, when translating "bread of life" (John 6:35) for a culture that did not have wheat-based loaves, some translators rendered the phrase "rice cake of life."

- Though "rice cake of life" may sound unusual to us, do you think this is an effective and accurate translation? Does it communicate an eternal truth *better* than talking about wheat bread in a culture where people aren't familiar with it? Does it correctly communicate the eternal life-giving nature of Christ? Explain your opinion.

- In general, do you think attempts to modernize biblical language or overcome cultural differences in language *hinder* the communication of the Bible's eternal truths or *enhance* its effectiveness? Explain.

The value of biblical language is in its origin and its effect.

God's Word is life governing and life giving. Read Deuteronomy 8:1–3. (Jesus quotes this passage in Matthew 4:4 when he is tempted by Satan.)

- How does Scripture feed and nourish you? Or, on the other hand, how does a lack of interaction with Scripture (due to busyness, poor priorities, and so on) leave you "underfed" or "malnourished" in a spiritual sense?

God's Word is divinely given. Throughout Scripture it is essential that God's people understand that the Scriptures are from God. This sounds simple, but consider how many times the prophets say, "Thus saith the Lord." Moses was clearly understood to be God's mouthpiece. Jeremiah said that God put his words in the prophet's mouth (Jer. 1:9).

- Imagine a non-Christian friend was curious about your beliefs about the Bible. How would you describe God's role in creating Scripture to your friend?

- Now imagine that same friend asked you, "What difference has the Bible made in your life?" What would you say? Share at least one specific example of a way the Bible has influenced your choices, attitudes, or actions.

Going Forward

Form pairs to discuss these questions:

- Van Leeuwen makes a strong case for his belief that a new, more direct translation of the Bible is needed. In light of all you've read and discussed, what's your reaction to Van Leeuwen's assertion? Do you agree or disagree? Why?

According to Wycliffe Bible Translators, more than 2,200 distinct language groups don't have a Bible in their own language. That's about 200 million people.

- How does this reality affect your own attitude toward your access to Scripture? Do you take it for granted? Explain.

- What issues has this study raised for you that will affect the way you'll read Scripture and approach Bible translations in the future?

Pray together for the scholars and translators at work today rendering Scripture into different languages as well as updating English translations. Pray for wisdom and discernment as they seek to communicate God's eternal truths across cultural barriers.

Notes

With so many competing claims about Christ in this world, how can a Christian distinguish between sound teaching and heresy?

SCRIPTURE FOCUS

- 1 Timothy 4:15–16
- 2 Timothy 4:2–5
- Titus 1:10–2:1

SESSION 4

WHAT'S AT STAKE?

Church history contains some brutal images: people who claimed to follow Christ being burned at the stake (or drowned or beheaded) by others who *also* claimed to follow Christ. The charge? Heresy. It was a very serious matter—so serious that leaders went to the unbiblical extreme of executing those they perceived to be spreading pernicious teachings.

Is heresy just a thing of the past? In most churches the word is hardly mentioned—it's rather out of place in our culture of tolerance. Yet as you'll explore in this study, many ancient heresies are alive and well today, just with different names and new angles. So how can a Christian distinguish between quasi-Christian ideas and true orthodox Christianity? In this study you'll examine how the early church leaders used Scripture as their authoritative guide to define Christian orthodoxy and you'll discuss how God's Word can serve as your guide as you distinguish between modern heresies and eternal truth.

■ Before You Meet

Read "Heresy in the Early Church: Sifting Through the Christ Controversies" from *Christian History & Biography*.

HERESY IN THE EARLY CHURCH:
SIFTING THROUGH THE CHRIST CONTROVERSIES

A quick summary of the competing schools of thought.

by the editors of Christian History & Biography

What matters were at the heart of the early church's battles against heresy? Many distinctions they made are difficult to translate into English. Still, all parties agreed on one thing: God is impassible; that is, he not subject to change or feelings. But how do you combine this with the Scriptures that imply Christ "became" human and suffered?

In particular, Christians argued passionately about two things:

1. Is Jesus Divine or Human?

• Christ Is Fully Divine!

Most of these people were driven by the conviction that only God can save humankind. Thus they were willing to protect the deity of Christ, even at the expense of his humanity, or in the case of the modalists, at the expense of the Trinity of persons.

Docetists, e.g., Gnostics: The divine Christ would never stoop to touch flesh, which is evil. Jesus only seemed (*dokeo*, in Greek) human and only appeared to die, for God cannot die. Or, in other versions, "Christ" left "Jesus" before the crucifixion. *Key text:* Phil. 2:8: " . . . and [Christ] being found in appearance as a man . . ." (all quotations in NIV).

Apollinarians: Jesus is not equally human and divine but one person with one nature. In Jesus's human flesh resided a divine mind and will (he didn't have a human mind or spirit), and his divinity controlled or sanctified his humanity. *Key text:* John 1:14: "The Word became flesh" (and not a human mind or will).

Modalists, a.k.a. Sabellians: God's names (Father, Son, Holy Spirit) change with his roles or "modes of being" (like a chameleon). When God is the Son, he is not the Father. There is no permanent distinction between the three "persons" of the Trinity, otherwise you have three gods. *Key texts:* Ex. 20:3: "You shall have no other gods before me" and John 10:30: "I and the Father are one."

• Christ May Be Special, But He's Not Divine!

These people took seriously the Gospels' portrait of Christ, in which Jesus is portrayed very much as a human being.

Ebionites: For these conservative Jewish Christians, God is one, and Jesus must be understood in Old Testament categories. Jesus was merely a specially blessed prophet. *Key text:* 1 Tim. 2:5: "For there is one God and one mediator between God and men, the man Jesus Christ."

Adoptionists, a.k.a., Dynamic Monarchianists: No denying Jesus was special, but what happened is this: at birth (not conception) or baptism, God "adopted" the human Jesus as his special son and gave him an extra measure of divine power (*dynamis*, in Greek). *Key text:* Luke 3:22 (in some ancient versions): "You are my beloved Son, today I have begotten you."

Arians: The Son as Word, Logos, was created by God before time. He is not eternal or perfect like God, though he was God's agent in creating everything else. *Key text*: John 1:14: "The Word [is] the only-begotten of the Father."

2. How is Jesus Both Divine and Human?

• Christ: One Nature!

Monophysites, e.g., Eutychians: Jesus cannot have two natures; his divinity swallowed up his humanity "like a drop of wine in the sea." *Key text:* Col. 1:19: "For God was pleased to have all his fullness dwell in him."

• Christ: Two Persons!

Nestorians: If you dismiss Jesus's humanity like that, he cannot be the Savior of humankind. Better to say he has two natures and also two persons: the divine Christ and the human Christ lived together in Jesus.

Key text: John 2:19: "Destroy this temple and I will raise it up in three days" (i.e., though the human Christ will be destroyed, the divine Christ will continue).

• The Orthodox View

Jesus is fully human and fully divine, having two natures in one person—"without confusion, without change, without division, without separation." *Key text:* Phil. 2:5–11: "Christ Jesus . . . being in very nature God, [was] made in human likeness . . . and become obedient to death. . . . Every tongue [should] confess Jesus Christ is Lord."

Open Up

Select one of these activities to launch your discussion time.

Option 1

Discuss these icebreaker questions:

- What's the weirdest thing you've ever heard a non-Christian claim about God or Jesus?
- What's the strangest thing you've heard someone who claims to be a Christian say about God or Jesus?
- Would you call either of these people's beliefs *heresy*? Why or why not?

Option 2

Play a few rounds of a simplified version of Balderdash. Pick an emcee for the game; he or she should flip through the dictionary and find an odd word. Everyone should write down that word on a piece of paper and then craft a made-up dictionary definition. The emcee should write the correct definition.

The emcee should then collect all the papers (including the real definition), shuffle them all, then read them aloud. Everyone gets to take one guess at which definition is the correct one; at the end, the emcee should reveal the right answer.

After playing for five to ten minutes, talk about these questions:

- Did you use the process of elimination in your decision making? If so, which false definitions did you eliminate right away? Why?
- What factors do you normally consider when you evaluate claims and beliefs that people have about Christ, the Church, or the Bible? What do you look to for your "definition" of what's essential to orthodox Christian belief?

In this study we'll explore how we define Christian orthodoxy and how we employ the "process of elimination" when we exclude certain beliefs or interpretations from that definition.

The Issue

Elaine Pagels, a religious historian who's questioned the exclusion of Gnostic texts from the biblical canon, has asked, "Who made that selection, and for what reasons? Why were these other writings excluded and banned as 'heresy'?" Pagels and other neo-Gnostics promote many of the same ideas of Gnosticism that have been popularized by books like *The Da Vinci Code.* (You'll look at Gnosticism more closely in Session 6.)

But Gnosticism isn't the only ancient heresy that's been popping up its head in recent years. Gwen Shamblin, founder of the Weigh-Down Workshop (a Christian alternative to dieting) has been accused of heresy for her teachings about the Trinity. According to CT's "Weighty Matters" by Elesha Coffman (September 2000),

> [Shamblin] writes in her doctrinal statement, "I believe that Jesus and God are two separate beings." She also objects to the term *trinity*: "Our feeling is that the word 'trinity' implies equality in leadership, or shared Lordship. . . . We feel that we grieve Jesus when we do not watch our words and their meaning—especially a word not found in either the Old or New Testament, writings that span centuries of God's inspired word."

Coffman notes the similarity between Shamblin's views and those of Arius, writing,

> Arius (ca. 250–ca. 336) disagreed with a different term, *homoousios*, which is a Greek word meaning "of the same substance"—as in, Jesus is "of the same substance" as the Father. Arius preferred *homoiousios*, "of similar substance" (making the proverbial one iota of difference). In song, he put it this way: "Yet the Son's substance is / Removed from the substance of the Father: / The Son is not equal to the Father, / Nor does he share the same substance."

When Shamblin's views came to light, her publisher (who, in full disclosure, is the same publisher of this small group guide) cancelled plans for an upcoming book, and many labeled Shamblin a heretic. Apologist L. L. "Don" Veinot, who spoke with Shamblin as the controversy erupted, told CT,

> "When I asked about her statement that the Father and Son are two separate beings, her reply was 'absolutely,'" Veinot says. "Her views are closer to that of Jehovah's Witnesses than anything resembling the historic biblical faith . . . The material on the Web site makes a distinction between the Father and Son that is heretical. She is clearly anti-Trinitarian." ("Gwen in the Balance," *Christianity Today*, October 2000)

- Do you agree that Shamblin's view on the Trinity is heretical? Why or why not?

Take a moment to scan back through the "Heresy in the Early Church" timeline and Christ controversy summaries, underlining any of the ideas you see that are still around today (perhaps in a new form). Consider ways these ancient heresies may still pop up within the church, as part of splinter groups or cults, or within the larger culture.

- Which heresies did you highlight? What forms do they take today?

Reflect

Take a moment to read 1 Timothy 4:15–16, 2 Timothy 4:2–5, and Titus 1:10–2:1. What are the key words and phrases in each passage? How do these passages address the issue of heresy? What questions do they raise for you?

Let's Explore

The health and future of the church, and therefore the gospel, depends upon correct teaching in the church.

- In what ways were you taught the basics of the faith, either as a child or a new (adult) believer?

In the Great Commission, Jesus commanded the disciples to share the Good News throughout the world, making new followers of Christ. Jesus called the disciples to "Teach them to obey everything that I have taught you" (Matthew 28:20).

- Which teachings of Jesus do you think are most important for the church to communicate to new Christians? What's the danger of not adequately teaching these truths?

Read 2 Timothy 4:2–5 and Titus 1:10–2:1.

- Which aspects of 2 Timothy 4:2–5 and Titus 1:10–2:1 do you think relate particularly well to the church today? Explain.

The Bible is the authoritative foundation for orthodoxy.

The Bible defines for us what is orthodox; after all, *orthodoxy* simply means "right teaching." But our understanding of what is orthodox Christianity also serves as a guide to help us properly *interpret* Scripture.

Briefly review together some of the heretical views presented in "Heresy in the Early Church: Sifting Through the Christ Controversies" and take turns reading aloud the key texts cited. Each of these heresies did use Scripture as a foundation for their belief, but their interpretation of Scripture was deemed incorrect.

- Which heretical interpretations strike you as way off-base? Which, if any, seem like they're just slightly off from the truth? Why?

- Are we free to derive our own meaning from Scripture in reliance on the Holy Spirit? Or do you think it's dangerous for people to try to interpret Scripture on their own without a clear sense of traditional orthodox Christian beliefs? Explain.

The sixty-six books of the Bible were written over many centuries by numerous authors in different contexts, using various literary styles (narrative, poetry, etc.). Questions emerge, such as: What is the overarching message of the Bible? How do the various parts of the Bible reveal God's truth? What is the coherent center of the Bible's message? What does the Bible teach as a whole about such issues as God and creation and sin and salvation (and not just its individual parts)? These questions call for Spirit-led discernment and theological reflection. One of the reasons the church has created creeds and confessions of faith throughout its history is to provide a "key" for understanding and interpreting Scripture.

In a *Books & Culture* article called "What Heresy?," writer and speaker Frederica Matthewes-Green explains her view on the importance of the historical Christian creeds this way:

> Say that it's like going to Paris. Everyone takes a photo of the Eiffel Tower. When we get home, we compare them; some snapshots are fuzzy and some from funny angles, but we can recognize them as depicting the same thing. The snaps don't capture the reality; nothing can; but they're okay as records.
>
> The Creeds are photos everyone agreed on. They are minimal and crisply focused, not fancied-up. They are not a substitute for personal experience but a useful guide for comparison, for discernment. If someone's snap shows King Kong climbing up the Tower, we can say, "Hey, you're off base there. Something's messing with your head." If Kong is wearing a lei and a paper party hat we might say, "Aw, now you're just making stuff up."

- Does your church use confessions of faith, creeds, or doctrinal statements as a way to teach the faith and to clarify your church's stance on issues? If so, what do you know or remember about them? Why are they important to your church?

- Some Christians believe that *only* Scripture is authoritative and that humanly created confessions or creeds should not ever be used. They are concerned that in some churches creeds or confessions are elevated too highly, as a near replacement to Scripture or revered as if equal to Scripture. Do you agree or disagree with this perspective? Why?

One of the great debates of the church has to do with what is essential to the faith and what is elective. In some cases, two people may disagree on a "gray area" of Scripture or Christian living but both come to conclusions that are within the bounds of orthodox Christianity. But in other matters two people may disagree, with one's conclusion being sound doctrine while the other's conclusion is heretical.

- What doctrines immediately come to mind for you as central and therefore can't be compromised? What doctrines or interpretations of the faith do you think are open to differences of interpretation?

God calls us to zealously protect our doctrine from the influence of the evil one.

- Recall the modern forms of ancient heresies you discussed earlier in the study. On a scale of 1 to 10 (1 being "harmless" and 10 being "ruinous"), how dangerous are they? Talk together about some specific examples.

The history of the church demonstrates the zeal with which church leaders fought heresy, often in a manner *far* from biblical: by burning heretics at the stake (and other horrific types of torture and execution). Both Catholic and Protestant church leaders over the centuries have been responsible for the execution of those they felt to be heretics.

- Has the pendulum swung too far the *other* way? Is the church now too permissive or tolerant toward heresies? Have we become too "nice" on this matter? Explain your point of view.

Read 1 Timothy 4:15–16.

- What does it really mean for an individual Christian to "watch" or "guard" his doctrine? What behaviors or practices might this involve? How do you apply this principle in your own life?

■ Going Forward

Discuss these final questions as a group:

Evangelical missiologist Paul Hiebert has said that there are two different models for thinking about group identity and belonging in the church: the one he calls a *centered-set approach* which draws people together on the basis of what is central to the faith and what people have in common with each other; the other he calls a *bounded-set approach*, which focuses on what excludes or includes people—on beliefs and behaviors that either get people accepted or rejected. Although it is over-simplified, traditionally evangelicals tend more toward a centered-set approach, whereas fundamentalists have used a bounded-set approach to understanding church.

- Do you favor a centered-set approach, emphasizing what most Christians have in common with each other? Or would you feel more comfortable with a bounded-set approach? Which model is more characteristic of your congregation?

Evangelical theologian Alister McGrath says it is necessary for any religious group to define itself in relation to other religious groups or in relation to society as a whole (*The Genesis of Doctrine*, Basil Blackwell).

Doctrine is a clarification of what the church believes or doesn't believe and a way of defining itself to others. Such doctrinal definitions help determine who is in and who is outside the group, and sets the conditions for getting into the group. To become a Christian assumes that one has a change of "social location."

McGrath's comments are insightful, but they run into a problem in our modern democratic society: we don't like to exclude anyone. It seems inhospitable and undemocratic.

- How can we extend hospitality and grace toward others who disagree with basic Christian convictions, yet still be clear about what we believe and how we live? Brainstorm specific ideas that relate to your church congregation and your small group.

Pray together, affirming your key beliefs about God. If you feel comfortable, consider concluding your prayer time by reciting the Nicene Creed.

THE NICENE CREED

I believe in one God, the Father Almighty, Maker of heaven and earth, and of all things visible and invisible.

And in one Lord Jesus Christ, the only-begotten Son of God, begotten of the Father before all worlds; God of God, Light of Light, very God of very God; begotten, not made, being of one substance with the Father, by whom all things were made.

Who, for us men and for our salvation, came down from heaven, and was incarnate by the Holy Spirit of the virgin Mary, and was made man; and was crucified also for us under Pontius Pilate; He suffered and was buried; and the third day He rose again, according to the Scriptures; and ascended into heaven, and sits on the right hand of the Father; and He shall come again, with glory, to judge the quick and the dead; whose kingdom shall have no end.

And I believe in the Holy Ghost, the Lord and Giver of Life; who proceeds from the Father and the Son; who with the Father and the Son together is worshipped and glorified; who spoke by the prophets.

And I believe one holy catholic and apostolic Church. I acknowledge one baptism for the remission of sins; and I look for the resurrection of the dead, and the life of the world to come. Amen.

When it comes to matters about which the Bible is unclear, silent, or its message is disputed, how can we develop God-honoring personal convictions?

SCRIPTURE FOCUS

- John 6:5–14
- Romans 14:1–15:3
- 1 Corinthians 8:1–15

SESSION 5

GRAY AREAS OF FAITH

Christians disagree. The existence of about thirty-nine thousand Christian denominations around the globe attests to this fact. But how do we handle disagreements over things Scripture doesn't cover? Or what about the issues that divide denominations—the issues about which each side finds sufficient biblical evidence to defend their position? Can Scripture still guide us when we aren't certain what the Bible really says about some matters? How should we arrive at our own personal convictions? And how can we maintain our individual beliefs while encouraging others to develop their own personal convictions?

Before You Meet

Read "Gray Matters" from *Christianity Today*.

GRAY MATTERS

How can we maintain our own convictions without imposing them on others?

by Ronald T. Habermas

Should Christians fight in wars; listen to rock music; support public schools; attend R-rated movies? What do these apparently unrelated items have in common? Each is a "gray area" under debate in some contemporary Christian community.

Gray areas are anything but novel. The early church at Rome was fractured by two prominent controversies: arguments about diet and arguments about holy days. The so-called weaker brothers favored a vegetarian diet, while the "stronger" believers boasted that any food was right to eat (Rom. 14:2). Similarly, the weaker brothers revered certain days more than others, while the stronger ones considered every day equally important (or, perhaps, equally unimportant).

Today, most Christians dismiss these controversies as irrelevant. In their place, however, some have substituted controversies over contemporary music, dress and hairstyles, and (I hear of at least one European fellowship) the drinking of Coca-Cola. But before we move quickly to cast our votes on these controversies (or to judge our fellow Christians), it is worth noting two things:

First, in Scripture, "weak" does not necessarily mean "bad," and "strong" does not necessarily mean "good." In another context, Paul admitted, "For we are glad, when we are weak, and ye are strong" (2 Cor. 13:9; all quotations in this article from the King James Version or the New Revised American Version). Perhaps the best translation for "weak" would be "dependent," that is, dependent on the structure provided by regulations.

Second, after explaining both sides of the diets-and-days controversies, Paul neither condemns nor condones the beliefs of either the strong or the weak. While we, along with first-century believers, want to know the right choice in every situation, the apostle seems more interested in other things: the unity of the church as well as the viability of individual preferences and convictions in the body.

We can be sure that similar controversies will exist until the Lord returns. But if the contemporary church is to cope effectively with these differences of opinion, it must learn from the experience of the early church recorded in Romans 14 and 1 Corinthians 8. These two chapters give us the wisdom we need to face three tragic failures.

Alternatives

The first failure we must face is our failure to teach alternatives within the faith.

Consider four basic positions that are usually offered as "alternatives" in a discussion of a "gray area." (I will use, as an example, the choices many of us face when subscribing to cable television and bringing into our homes material that may be more questionable than the Disney Channel. If you have your mind made up about that one, just substitute the more arcane controversy over Coca-Cola.)

First comes the mature participant, the one who says, "I have a clear conscience about having a mixture of good and bad programming coming into my home. I believe I can make good choices while avoiding a superior attitude toward other believers who do not share my conviction."

Second is the mature non-participant. This person says, "I do not have a clear conscience about subscribing to these cable channels. I do not trust my own self-control. However, I try not to condemn those who permit it."

Third is the immature participant, the one who says, "I watch any cable TV movie that I please. The church does not have the authority to tell me what not to do."

Fourth comes the immature non-participant. This person says, "I don't watch any movies or TV. In fact, no true Christian would ever bring such material into his home."

From Romans 14, we can see that only the two viewpoints we've labeled "mature" are alternatives for the believer. Unfortunately, it is often the dominant rule of the immature positions that threatens personal freedom and retards maturation among believers. The church must assist its members in comprehending the broad range of acceptable options, encouraging "divergent learning" (considering all viable options) in the place of "convergent learning" (accepting only limited, predetermined responses).

The early church father Gregory Thaumaturgus recounts his own training under Origen: "No subject was forbidden us, nothing hidden or inaccessible. We were allowed to become acquainted with every doctrine, barbarian or Greek, with things spiritual and secular, divine and human, traversing with all confidence and investigating the whole circuit of knowledge, and satisfying ourselves with full enjoyment of all pleasure of the soul."

While these church fathers distinguished between truth and error, they made a point of investigating everything. We must also, for the spirit that investigates never becomes unduly narrow, while the soul that seeks only safe answers fast becomes pinched and primly pious.

Our spiritual forefathers learned the secret of implementing the maxim "All truth is God's truth." To emulate their example, we must strike a balance in two areas:

First, we must maintain a tension between "investigation" and "experimentation." On the one hand, believers do not need to experience drunkenness to know it is sinful. In grayer areas, however, some experimentation is warranted.

Second, there is a tension between acknowledging the boundaries of one's personal convictions and adjusting those beliefs—either more rigidly or loosely—in light of other believers' convictions (a balance between the "individual" and the "corporate"). For instance, I knew a woman who was convicted about reading a popular news magazine because of its consistently liberal worldview, which often conflicted with her Christian standards and values. She refrained from reading this literature until she discovered her pastor subscribed to it. Encouraged by his example, she once again attempted to read the weekly publication, only to experience further conviction. In time she realized that the solution to her dilemma was not to dismiss her commendable desire to be informed about world events, but to substitute for her present reading a more conservative news publication.

Convictions

The second failure with which we must deal is our failure to encourage personal convictions. The philosophical tendencies of our society encourage personal decisions but often without reference to the question of truth. It's a matter of "what works for you." Without getting lost in this existential morass, Christians must learn to ask, "Given all the options within the boundaries of faith, what do I believe?" This challenge requires a commitment to help others make faith choices.

Making personal choices is never easy, for there is the constant temptation to mimic blindly someone else's beliefs. "I follow what my pastor preaches" and "I observe what my parents taught me" are not adequate responses for the mature believer, since these attitudes betray a failure to analyze the why and how of personal convictions.

What does the apostle say about making personal faith choices? Four significant themes can be cited from Romans 14.

First, Paul says, "Let every man be fully persuaded in his own mind" (v. 5b). The root word for *fully persuaded* suggests literally a container filled to the brim, and metaphorically a person thoroughly convinced. Paul employs the same word to describe Abraham's faith in God's promises (Rom. 4; 19–21).

Second, Paul makes an explosive statement: What may be appropriate for one person may be totally inappropriate for another. Situational ethics? No, but Paul realized (like Jesus in Mark 7) that evil is in people, not so much in things. So he writes, "I know and am persuaded in the Lord Jesus that nothing is unclean in itself" (Rom. 14:14a NRSV). Yet the author adds, "But it is unclean for any one who thinks it is unclean" (v. 14b NRSV). This seeming contradiction was resolved in Paul's mind when each believer exercised his God-given freedom in discerning the limits of his own conscience.

The third theme Paul raises is the blessedness of the person who is fully convinced in his belief: "Happy is he who has no reason to judge himself for what he approves" (v. 22b). "Happy" (as *makarios* is rendered in the King James and Revised Standard versions) is an unfortunately narrow translation, since Paul's phraseology ("Blessed is he who . . .") is typical of the way the Jewish wisdom tradition spoke of the objects of God's favor and their resulting well-being. Elsewhere Paul uses the same word to speak of those who have their sins forgiven and those who endure temptation (hardly a "happy" situation). For Paul, then, the person who is fully convinced and acts on his convictions is the one who finds God's behavior and experiences well-being.

Finally, Paul claims that the person who has doubts about a "gray area" but who participates anyway, is actually condemning himself (v. 23a).

I knew a young man (I'll call him Steve) who was an extraordinarily talented musician. After his conversion, several of us from the congregation regularly encouraged Steve to adapt some of his contemporary music for our church services. Steve routinely balked at the invitations. But one day this new convert gave in to our requests. In the lobby following the evening service in which Steve had contributed skills, I noticed he was despondent. From the dialogue that ensued, I learned that Steve was not so much offended by the contemporary music per se, but by the sinful practices that had accompanied it in his previous lifestyle. We had selfishly and unwittingly pushed this young Christian to a point of self-condemnation by denying the significance of his own convictions before God.

The critical feature of Paul's statement in Romans 14 is not that the person has sinned through his overt behavior (in this case, eating meat), but from the lack of conviction that it is good to act this way. He did not act on his own faith, but on the faith of another. It was surrogate faith. Or it was unstable faith, as James wrote (using the same word for *doubting*), "The one who doubts is like a wave of the sea driven and tossed by the wind" (1:6b NRSV).

For Paul, a person is either possessed by a settled faith or by fluctuating doubts. Sin is not in things (like food or days), but in people. Sin is not only in overt actions (for some acts are indeed harmful), but in lack of conviction, as he writes, "For whatever does not proceed from faith is sin" (Rom. 14:23 NRSV).

Thus the church must emphasize to the members the importance of making personal faith choices. And the cultivation of decision-making skills must be a substantial part of the educating process.

Responsibility

The third failure is the failure to couple freedom with responsibility. Unrestricted freedom leads to anarchy and irresponsibility. In Romans 14, the apostle describes two kinds of restrictions: duties based on our relationship to God and duties imposed by our responsibility to others.

Part of our duty to God is to avoid usurping his roles. Thus, Paul writes, we must respect God's action in four areas: First, regardless of a believer's choice with respect to a given gray area, "God hath received him" (v. 3b KJV). Next, all believers are ultimately responsible to God—not to one another. Paul asks, "Who art thou that judgest another man's servant?" (v. 4a KJV). We are to mind our own business and let God mind his. Third, God will assist each believer in standing up for his own convictions (v. 4b). Finally, it is Christ himself who is Lord of the church (v. 9). We must let him rule it.

Paul also asks us to respect other believers in four ways: First, just as God has accepted all of his children (regardless of their stands on gray areas), believers must also accept one another (v. 1). We must deliberately learn to trust other believers, especially those who select ethical positions that differ from ours. That is the positive attitude to which Paul calls us. Next comes the command to abandon a negative attitude: believers must stop judging those who have alternative convictions (vv. 3, 13a). Third, Christians must give the benefit of the doubt to fellow believers (vv. 6–7). No believers should be so presumptuous as to think he is the only one dedicated to the work of the Lord. Rather, he must believe that people on both sides of gray issues take their stands in service of the Lord. Finally, Paul stresses the need for a Christian to avoid becoming a "stumbling block" (vv. 15–21).

Paul's statements about stumbling blocks have triggered much discussion. "What constitutes a legitimate example of a stumbling block?" we want to know. In the two critical passages, Romans 14 and

1 Corinthians 8, we find five critical components that combine to form a stumbling-block chain of events:

Component 1: The stronger believer performs an activity that may be ethically questionable for others, but is permissible for him (see 1 Cor. 8:3–8).

Component 2: The weaker brother observes the stronger one participating in this activity, which he himself does not have a clear conscience to indulge in (1 Cor. 8:10a).

Component 3: Desiring the same freedom, the weaker brother follows the lead of his stronger counterpart (1 Cor. 8:10b).

Component 4: Because the weaker brother has not acted upon his own conviction (but upon the conviction of his stronger model), his conscience is "wounded" and he becomes "grieved" (1 Cor. 8:12; Rom. 14:15). The word translated "grieved" is the same word used to describe the disciples' reaction when they heard Jesus say he would be betrayed by one of them (Matt 26:22). And the same word described Jesus's own experience in Gethsemane (Matt. 26:37). Clearly, the stumbling-block sequence is more than a superficial difference of opinion. It involves a severe emotional disturbance on the part of the weaker Christian.

Component 5: The stronger believer is informed (probably by the weaker Christian) that he is responsible for the condition grieving his brother.

Only when all five components are present is a stronger believer becoming a stumbling block to the weaker one. And in these cases, there are two obligations. The weaker is obligated to let the stronger know how the questionable behavior is affecting him. And the stronger has the obligation to curtail his liberty for the sake of the weaker one's conscience.

Pursuing Peace

In ancient Rome and Corinth, interpersonal differences obscured people's vision of the big goal God had set for them—the need to value and promote harmonious relationships in the body of Christ. Concerns over diet and holy days made them forget the importance of church unity and their responsibilities to maturing believers. It would be sad indeed if we—who have the benefit of apostolic wisdom—let petty controversies cause us to miss the big issues.

Jesus said that the world would know his followers by their love for one another. Exercising love today certainly means educating believers about the breadth of options; it certainly means encouraging believers to come to personal convictions; and, without doubt, it means letting our respect for God and our respect for fellow believers limit our personal freedom. Exercising love this way will help us reclaim "unity in diversity" and enhance our witness to a watching world.

Ronald Habermas is professor and chair of biblical studies and Christian formation at John Brown University. He is the author of many journal articles and several books including The Complete Disciple *(Chariot Victor) and* Introduction to Christian Education and Formation *(Zondervan). "Gray Matters" was first published in* Christianity Today, *August 1987, page 23.*

■ Open Up

Select one of these activities to launch your discussion time.

Option 1

Discuss these icebreaker questions:

- What's one thing that you think a Christian should never do? Now imagine someone whose viewpoint is more theologically conservative than your own. What's something he or she might say a Christian should never do?
- What are the main lifestyle and behavior issues about which Christians disagree? (For example, should a Christian drink alcohol?) Brainstorm six to ten issues together.
- There are also many theological and biblical matters about which Bible-believing Christians disagree. Brainstorm six to ten issues together.

Option 2

You'll need four pieces of poster board (or four large sheets of paper), four black markers, and four red markers for this activity. Form four equal-sized teams (if needed, a team can be one person). Each team needs a poster and a black and red marker.

Take five to seven minutes to follow these instructions in your group:

Team 1: Brainstorm together and list as many *theological* "gray areas" as you can. Use your black marker to list issues that all your team members believe are gray areas. Use your red marker to list theological issues that your team members don't all agree are gray or to add issues that you know other Christians may consider to be gray.

Team 2: Brainstorm together and list *theological* issues that you believe are "black and white"—that are non-negotiable truths and beliefs made clear in Scripture. Use your black marker to list theological issues that all your team members agree are black and white areas. Use your red marker to list theological issues that only some in your team consider black and white or to add issues that you know other Christians may consider black and white.

Team 3: Brainstorm together and list as many "gray areas" as you can in the realm of *lifestyle choices* or *behaviors*. Use your black marker to write issues that all your team members agree are gray areas. Use your red marker to list behavioral issues that your team members don't all agree to be gray or to add lifestyle choices which you know other Christians may consider to be gray.

Team 4: Brainstorm together and list *lifestyle choices* or *behaviors* that you believe are "black and white"—that are direct teachings made clear in Scripture. Use your black marker to list lifestyle matters that your entire team agrees are black and white. Use your red marker to list behavioral choices that only some in your team view as black and white or to add issues that you know other Christians might consider to be black and white.

When you're done, gather together as a whole group and briefly present each of the posters, explaining your team's assignment. Take a moment to write additional ideas on each other's posters, then talk about these questions:

- Are there any black and white issues listed on the posters that you consider to be gray? If so, what are they?
- Are there any gray issues on the lists that you personally consider to be black and white? Explain.

Keep the posters in view during the study and refer to the lists you've generated as you discuss what Scripture has to say about this topic.

■ The Issue

In his article, Habermas alludes to the "broad range of acceptable options" for Christian practice and beliefs; he takes it as a given that there are allowable differences of opinion on a variety of matters which all remain "within the boundaries of faith."

- Do you agree that there are gray areas of Scripture? If so, how would you make your case to someone who believed that everything is black and white? If not, why not?

The notion that there are "gray areas" of Scripture is sometimes criticized because it can lead to a slippery-slope mentality. For example, if we say that some issues in the Bible are open to various interpretations, what's to stop someone from treating the entire Bible as if it could be interpreted any way one would like?

- What do you see as the key differences between acknowledging the existence of "gray areas" in Scripture versus having an "anything goes" mentality about lifestyle choices and biblical interpretation? Share examples to explain your answer.

Reflect

Take a moment to read and reflect on John 16:5–15, Romans 14:1–15:3, and 1 Corinthians 8:1–13. Take note of the central ideas in each passage, writing down key words and phrases. Consider how these passages speak to the issue of gray areas.

Let's Explore

Scripture serves as our guide even on matters that aren't directly addressed in the Bible.

What does it really mean to assert that something is a gray area of Scripture? It does not mean that the Bible is confused or somehow schizophrenic, holding opposing positions simultaneously. It does not mean that people can interpret Scripture to say anything they want. And it does not mean that believers can select only some biblical teachings to believe and reject others.

- From your own personal thinking and study, share an example of a lifestyle or theological issue that *you* consider to be a gray area. In your opinion, why is it gray? Explain your rationale.

If we believe the Bible is the authoritative word of God, then careful, responsible study can enable us to draw conclusions about areas that are not directly addressed in Scripture or about which God's Word may not be as clear as we'd like. The issue must be approached with the full context of God's Word in mind. We must avoid proof-texting—basing our stance on a gray area on just one verse that may be taken out of context. We must also not base our position on only an obscure or confusing text, lest we conclude something outside the realm of Christian orthodoxy. For example, Mormons believe in the practice of baptizing on behalf of the dead and the justification for this doctrine is based on two obscure texts, 1 Corinthians 15:29 and 1 Peter 4:6. Though these passages are definitely part of God's authoritative and infallible Word for us, when unusual phrases are isolated and entire theological viewpoints are built upon them outside of the rest of the counsel of God's Word, as in this example, the conclusion that results can be wrong. Instead, when considering gray areas, we must gather general principles consistently presented in Scripture as the foundation for our decision-making.

There are many, many ethical issues and lifestyle choices that face Christians today which aren't directly addressed in Scripture (such as Internet use, birth control, file-sharing of downloaded music, political parties, smoking, R-rated movies, green energy, and so on). Yet as Christians we must still look to the Bible for the guiding principles to help us make decisions on these matters.

- As a group, name one issue facing modern Christians that's not addressed in Scripture (from the above list or your own idea), then discuss the biblical principles that you think could apply to that matter. What should a Christian consider in making up his or her mind about this issue?

We can navigate gray areas by heeding the Holy Spirit's conviction of our hearts and guidance of our conscience.

Review the four alternative conclusions Habermas says Christians might draw about gray areas (page 79). Habermas concludes that only the first two alternatives are valid positions for a Christian to take; in his view, both the "immature participant" and the "immature non-participant" approaches are unbiblical responses.

- Do you agree with Habermas that only the first two alternatives are appropriate responses to a gray area? Why or why not?

- Which of these alternatives do you most often observe in your church? Have *you* ever held an immature participant or immature non-participant position? Explain.

Independence and personal freedom of choice are values deeply imbedded in our society. Perhaps the Rolling Stones encapsulated it best in their simple, catchy lyric: "I'm free to do what I want any old time!"

And to acknowledge the existence of gray areas *is* to acknowledge a degree of freedom for Christians to make their own determinations about particular matters. But Habermas contrasts the whatever-works-for-you philosophy of our society with a more responsible, soul-searching approach for Christians in making decisions about gray areas. He urges Christians to ask, "Given all the options within the boundaries of faith, what do I believe?"

We are not called to make this determination on our own, however. Read aloud John 16:5–15.

- According to this passage, what does the Holy Spirit do in our lives? How have you experienced this in your own life? Share an example.

Habermas shares the example of a young man named Steve who gave into peer pressure from Christian friends and went against his conscience in doing something the others considered harmless. Habermas writes, "We had selfishly and unwittingly pushed this young Christian to a point of self-condemnation by denying the significance of his own convictions before God."

The Apostle Paul focuses strongly on the significance of personal convictions on issues that we might aptly call matters of conscience. Review Romans 14, paying particular attention to verses 5, 12, 14, and 23.

- Have you ever felt a strong personal conviction about something that other Christian friends may not have shared? How did you handle that experience?

Habermas claims that "Sin is not only in overt actions (for some acts are indeed harmful), but in lack of conviction."

- What do you think he means? Do you agree with him? Why or why not?

We're called to make decisions about gray areas with the health of the Christian community in mind.

Not only do we have a duty toward God regarding gray areas, obeying his leading and answering to him for our conclusions, but Habermas says we must also consider the "duties imposed by our responsibility to others."

Review Romans 14:13, 19, 15:1–3; and 1 Corinthians 8:9–13.

- What's your gut reaction to these passages? What makes them so hard to live out?

The idea of not putting a stumbling block in the way of another believer can be taken to a legalistic extreme. If taken too far, it can end up prohibiting *any* freedom Christians might have. (For example, if a weaker Christian friend struggles with watching inappropriate content on cable television, does that mean that the other Christians in his church shouldn't have cable TV in order not to tempt that person and cause him to stumble? Or perhaps might it even mean that all the believers should give up watching television all together to help this "weaker brother"?)

In his article, Habermas draws on the principles of Romans 14–15 and 1 Corinthians 8 to clarify what he thinks constitutes a true "stumbling block." Review Habermas's five-component definition of a legitimate stumbling block (in the "Responsibility" section of his article.)

- Do you think Habermas's criteria for what constitutes a stumbling block are too strict, too loose, or just right? Are there other considerations you might add?

- When have you made a choice about a gray area out of consideration for others rather than purely based on your own convictions? (If you haven't done this, are there areas in your life in which you think you may need to do this?)

Going Forward

When it comes to gray areas, we each must develop a personal conviction about what we believe to be true in our interpretation of Scripture, regarding both theological ideas and lifestyle choices. Asserting that there are gray areas does not mean we believe multiple interpretations on a given matter to all be correct. After all, we hold our convictions because we believe the conclusions we've drawn about these matters to be the *right* ones.

Yet in this sense of conviction—this feeling of rightness—we must never embrace pride, arrogance, self-assuredness, or judgment of others. Instead, we're called to hold our positions on gray areas with humility and an attitude of grace toward Christians who've come to different conclusions.

- Without revealing specific names, describe encounters you've had with Christians whose sense of conviction about gray areas (either theological matters or lifestyle choices) was accompanied by arrogance, pride, or judgment. How did that person's demeanor affect you and others? How might it have impaired Christian unity or negatively affected that person's Christian witness?

Form pairs to discuss these final questions.

A centuries-old motto of the church, credited to many Christian thinkers and embraced by various Christian groups, speaks soundly and succinctly to this issue: "In essentials, unity; in non-essentials, liberty; in all things, charity."

- In light of what you've read and discussed, how do you feel called to grant greater liberty (freedom) to other believers? In what specific areas might you need to surrender legalism, pride, or a judgmental mind-set toward others?

- How can you practically show agape love (charity) to Christians who differ from you in their conclusions about gray areas? Share specific ideas of actions and attitudes that communicate true charity.

Pray with your partner about specific gray areas which you desire to look into and seek God's leading about. Also ask God to strengthen your willingness to surrender your own personal freedom, as needed, for the sake of other believers.

Why are many Christians uncritically embracing the ideas and teachings of Gnosticism?

SCRIPTURE FOCUS

Luke 1:1–4

John 1:1–7

Romans 3:10–23

1 Corinthians 15:1–8

SESSION 6

ARE THE GNOSTIC "GOSPELS" RELIABLE?

■

Christians of the early church saw Gnosticism, a religious movement that took root in the second century AD, as a threat to the historic Old Testament and Jesus's teaching. Gnosticism is making a comeback in our day through the so-called Gospel of Judas and *The Da Vinci Code*, which draws on extra-biblical documents as the base for its story line. What makes Gnosticism so dangerous is that it puts man at the center of the universe instead of God, a trend already popular among those who want a convenient and customized faith.

This study asks: Why did the early church reject the Gnostic gospels, and what are the major doctrinal differences between the Gnostic gospels and the biblical canon? Why aren't the Gnostic gospels relevant for today? Why are we so susceptible to Gnostic ideas?

Before You Meet

Read "Why the 'Lost Gospels' Lost Out" from *Christianity Today*.

WHY THE 'LOST GOSPELS' LOST OUT

Recent gadfly theories about church council conspiracies that manipulated the New Testament into existence are bad—really bad—history.

by Ben Witherington III

In Dan Brown's best-selling novel *The Da Vinci Code*, villain Leigh Teabing explains to cryptologist Sophie Neveu that at the Council of Nicea (AD 325) "many aspects of Christianity were debated and voted upon," including the divinity of Jesus. "Until that moment," he says, "Jesus was viewed by His followers as a mortal prophet . . . a great and powerful man, but a man nonetheless."

Neveu is shocked: "Not the Son of God?"

Teabing explains: "Jesus's establishment as 'the Son of God' was officially proposed and voted on by the Council of Nicea."

"Hold on. You're saying that Jesus's divinity was the result of a vote?"

"A relatively close one at that," Teabing says.

A little later, Teabing adds this speech: "Because Constantine upgraded Jesus's status almost four centuries *after* Jesus's death, thousands of documents already existed chronicling His life as a mortal man. To rewrite the history books, Constantine knew he would need a bold stroke . . . Constantine commissioned and financed a new Bible, which omitted those gospels that spoke of Christ's *human* traits and embellished those gospels that made Him godlike. The earlier gospels were outlawed, gathered up, and burned."

Unfortunately, this passage of fiction has raised questions for many readers because it appears to be an accurate historical summary embedded in an otherwise fictitious account. It is anything but that.

The novel expresses in popular form what some scholars have been arguing or implying for years. Twenty years ago, Elaine Pagels wrote *The Gnostic Gospels*, a book that introduced the larger public to the other "Christian" writings that arose in the early centuries of the church. Regarding the books of the New Testament, Pagels asked, "Who made that selection and for what reasons? Why were these other writings excluded and banned as 'heresy'?"

For Pagels this wasn't a rhetorical question, but one designed to get readers to question the very authority of the New Testament.

The issue of canon—what books constitute the final authority for Christians—is no small matter. If the critics are correct, then Christianity must indeed be radically reinterpreted, just as they suggest. If they are wrong, traditional Christians have their work cut out for them, because many seekers remain skeptical of claims to biblical authority.

Let us examine whether revisionist authors' claims stand up to the historical test.

'Heresy' in the Beginning

Pagels is a history of religions professor at Princeton University. Her book explores a number of ancient texts that teach Gnosticism—the collective name for many greatly varying sects that believed that matter is essentially evil and spirit good, and that God is infinitely divorced from the world.

Where Judaism and Christianity emphasize the role of faith and works in salvation, and salvation of both body and spirit, gnostics taught that the soul's salvation depended on the individual possessing quasi-intuitive knowledge (gnosis) of the mysteries of the universe and of magic formulas.

Pagels admits that the gnostic texts were rejected by the orthodox, but she claims that it wasn't until the period of great councils (325 and after) that "orthodoxy" was defined as opposed to "heresy." Thus fourth-century religious politics decided "orthodoxy." As one character in *The Da Vinci Code* puts it, "Anyone who chose the forbidden gospels over Constantine's version was deemed a heretic. The word *heretic* derives from that moment in history."

But was there really no such thing as "orthodoxy" before the fourth century? Is it really the case that Gnosticism was harshly suppressed without being given a fair trial?

First, there is no strong evidence to suggest that gnostic Christians vied with the orthodox from the beginning. Even what is probably the earliest gnostic document, the Gospel of Thomas, seems to have come from a period after the New Testament books were already recognized as authoritative and widely circulated.

The Gospel of Thomas, in fact, draws on most of these documents, adding some new ideas about Jesus and about the faith. All other major gnostic texts—like the Gospel of Truth, the Gospel of Philip, the Gospel of the Hebrews, the Gospel of Mary, and so on—are clearly written in the second and third centuries.

Church Fathers Irenaeus and Tertullian addressed Gnosticism in the second century in works titled *Against Heresies* and *The Prescription Against Heretics*. And the Muratorian Canon (a list of New Testament writings from late second century) says this: "There is current also an epistle to the Laodiceans, and another to the Alexandrians, both forged in Paul's name to further the heresy of Marcion, and several others which cannot be received into the catholic Church. For it is not fitting that gall be mixed with honey." In other words, it is historically false to say that the councils of the fourth and fifth centuries invented or first defined "heresy."

Revisionist historians like Pagels also argue that there was no core belief system, later called "orthodoxy," in the first century. This is a strange claim, because anyone who has read the letters of John, for example, knows that discussions about orthodoxy and heresy were heating up in the New Testament period. Paul's letters, too, show distinctions being made between truth and error. By the time we get to the Pastoral Epistles (1 and 2 Timothy, and Titus), there is a strong sense of what is and is not sound doctrine, particularly in terms of salvation and the person of Jesus Christ.

Furthermore, the early church viewed the Old Testament as both authoritative and inspired, as 2 Timothy 3:16 shows. This is an important point in regard to Gnosticism. The earliest churches had already recognized the Hebrew Scriptures as canon, a set of authoritative and divinely inspired texts. Notice how much of the Old Testament is quoted in the New Testament books—all written to edify churches across the ancient world. Gnosticism fundamentally rejected Jewish theology about the goodness of creation, and especially the idea that all the nations could be blessed through Abraham and his faith. When the church accepted the Hebrew Scriptures, it implicitly rejected Gnosticism before it had a chance to get started. Thus we are already at a watershed moment in the development of early Christianity, one that could not allow Gnosticism to ever be regarded as a legitimate development of the Christian faith.

New Testament scholar Pheme Perkins points out how rarely the Gnostic literature refers to the Old Testament: "Gnostic exegetes were only interested in elaborating their mythic and theological speculations concerning the origins of the universe, not in appropriating a received canonical tradition. . . . [By contrast] the Christian Bible originates in a hermeneutical framing of Jewish scriptures, so that they retain their canonical authority and yet serve as witnesses to the Christ-centered experience of salvation."

She puts her finger on one of the main reasons gnostic texts could never have been included in the canon—they largely rejected the Scriptures the earliest Christians affirmed, the Hebrew Bible.

The formation of authoritative apostolic texts, moreover, was already occurring in the New Testament period. We see this in 2 Peter 3:16, which says of Paul: "He writes this same way in all his letters, speaking in them of these matters. His letters contain some things that are hard to understand, which ignorant and unstable people distort, as they do the other Scriptures . . ." Even if this text was written in the earliest years of the second century (as some New Testament scholars think), it makes plain that there was already a collection of Paul's letters that were considered authoritative and on a par with "Scriptures."

In other words, by the New Testament period, there was already a core of documents and ideas by which Christians could evaluate other documents. The New Testament documents already manifest a concept of "orthodoxy," or at least criteria by which truth and error could be distinguished. Among the second-century lists of authoritative Scriptures, never are gnostic texts listed—not even by the unorthodox Marcion in about 140. There was never a time when a wide selection of books, including gnostic ones, was widely deemed acceptable.

A good example of this is Serapion of Antioch (a bishop from 190 to 211), who let some of his flock read the Gospel of Peter in church—until he read the book himself. He concluded that it had a heretical Christology, teachings about Jesus that did not conform to other ancient apostolic documents. Or compare the Apocalypse of Peter with the canonical gospel portraits of Jesus's Passion. The gnostic text depicts Jesus as glad and laughing on the cross, a radiant being of gnostic light (81:10–11).

Pagels's suggestions to the contrary, gnostic texts were never seriously entertained by many Christians as legitimate representations of the faith.

But wait a minute, say the critics. We don't have the original New Testament documents. All we have are copies of copies. What if there were orthodox monks who deliberately changed the text while copying it, shaping it according to their own theology, so that our New Testament is a far cry from the originals?

The Non-Problem of Copies

Though we have close to five thousand original-language manuscripts containing text from part or all of what we now call the New Testament, no two copies are exactly alike. The question for many, then, becomes whether there was some sort of conspiracy to change the originals to make them conform to the orthodoxy taught in the fourth- and fifth-century churches.

As noted earlier, this question has taken popular form in *The Da Vinci Code*, where "thousands of documents" supposedly chronicled Christ's life as "a mortal man." Constantine supposedly destroyed these gospels and "embellished" the four Gospels to make Christ appear more "godlike." Is there any truth to this?

Bart Ehrman is a specialist in New Testament text criticism—the study of partial and whole manuscripts to reconstruct original texts. In his *Orthodox Corruption of Scripture* (1997), Ehrman meticulously explores what he calls the orthodox corruptions of Scripture. This enables him to document how, in response to various heresies (including Gnosticism), some scribes added or subtracted from the text to highlight the true humanity or true divinity of Christ. I emphasize *highlight*, because Ehrman does not suggest, as *The Da Vinci Code* does, that new ideas were simply imported into the text. For example, sometimes the word *Christ* is added to the name Jesus to emphasize his exalted status even from birth. It is not as though a foreign idea is sneaking into the text. The vast majority of these enhancements are not to be found in our modern translations (NIV, NRSV, the New Living) because text critics have demonstrated they were not part of the originals.

The most important observation to be made is that none of the "corruptions" or corrections was carried out in a systematic way. We have no evidence of a systematic conspiracy by the orthodox church to doctor the text of the New Testament, particularly the Gospels, in order to prop up a new Christology. Yes, certain overzealous individuals, Ehrman shows, were even prepared to create forgeries to support their own view of orthodoxy. But well before the canonization of the New Testament, many Christians had the established apostolic testimony to evaluate the authority—or not—of the various copies floating about.

In fact, on the whole, Christian scribes were notably conservative in how they handled their copies. Worried that a verse might be misunderstood, sometimes they would seek to clarify that which could be overlooked, distorted, or misconstrued. Sometimes they would find alternate readings in the margins of the manuscripts they were copying from, and they would include both readings lest they leave out the correct one. These scribes had a profound sense that they were copying the sacred Scriptures, and they did not want to leave anything out that the originally inspired author had included.

If Ehrman had left his discussion at that point, there might not be any objection to his argument. But he goes on to plow the same furrow as Pagels and King; he too writes revisionist history, arguing for a wide array of beliefs at the church's beginning. The struggle over an emerging orthodoxy, in his view, was not solidified until the fourth century.

How much more solid Ehrman's book would be if it had come to grips with works by Martin Hengel that deal with both early Judaism and early Christianity. There could hardly be a scholar better grounded in primary source texts, both orthodox and heterodox.

From the outset of his *The Four Gospels and the One Gospel of Jesus Christ* (2000), Hengel stresses that "primitive Christianity has no knowledge of the abrupt distinction between theology and history: The truth lies between a 'historicism' which is hostile to theology, and a 'dogmatism' which is hostile to history."

Hengel shows that the titles on the canonical Gospels—"according to Matthew," and so on—likely were already in place by at least 125. This would mean they circulated together, because the titles imply a distinction between, for example, Luke's rendering and Mark's. Indeed, the collection of four Gospels together may have been one of the first such collections to circulate in one codex or book.

We can say without hesitation that various books that were to become part of the New Testament were already seen and used as authoritative and acceptable in the second century in various parts of the church, both Eastern and Western—and that their listing as authoritative in the early fourth century was without serious debate.

In the end, the gnostic gospels and other gnostic documents were never even considered for inclusion in the Christian canon. Other, non-gnostic books that did not make it into the canon were debated rather heavily—namely, the Shepherd of Hermas, 1 Clement, the letters of Ignatius, and, most surprisingly, the Wisdom of Solomon. It is noteworthy that not a single document written after about 120 was ever considered for inclusion in the canon, not least because such documents were not written by people in direct touch with the apostolic tradition, much less with the apostles themselves.

Hence, contrary to Pagels and others, the case was never that the gnostic documents were excluded or deleted. Rather, they were never serious contenders for inclusion in the canon, either in the Eastern or the Western church. As the canon list of Athanasius in 367 demonstrates, even in the home region of the Nag Hammadi texts none of those texts was ever included in a canon. None ever appeared in any authoritative list, and it is perhaps also suggestive that when the Nag Hammadi texts were found, they were found without one single canonical book included with them. This should tell us something about how they were separated from and viewed differently from canonical books.

The New Gnostic Faith

Some twenty years after she wrote *The Gnostic Gospels,* Elaine Pagels penned the beautifully written *Beyond Belief.* In a particularly candid and confessional part of the book, Pagels talks about how she had been alienated from Christian faith while in high school: She was part of an evangelical church when a Jewish friend died, and her fellow Christians told her that since the friend was not born again, she was going to hell.

Though this turned her off from the church, she maintained a lively interest in New Testament studies and the early church. While doing doctoral work at Harvard, she had an epiphany. She was reading the Gospel of Thomas when she came across this saying of Jesus: "If you bring forth what is within you, what you bring forth will save you."

She comments: "The strength of this saying is that it does not tell us what to believe but challenges us to discover what lies hidden within ourselves; and with a shock of recognition, I realized that this perspective seemed to me self evidently true."

Her comparison of the Gospel of Thomas and the Gospel of John reveals how far down this road she has traveled. In John, there is an "I-and-Thou" relationship, a vine and branches relationship, that involves an integral connection between the divine and human without identification of the "I" with the "Thou." But in Thomas, it is a matter of "I am Thou." The self is deified and is seen as the finish line of faith.

Here we find the appeal to personal impressions or experience as the final authority. The believer is not asked to believe specific things that come from without (by revelation), nor to submit to any authority but the self. Instead, we are to be the measure of ourselves and to find our own truths within us.

In this book, we see Pagels's story of suffering and feeling betrayed, and her long spiritual journey to a reconfigured form of Christianity—

reconfigured as self-actualization. And it is evident that the gnostic texts have helped lead her in that direction.

Pagels is not a disinterested scholar when she writes about Gnosticism. Her spiritual journey entices her to look at the gnostic texts in a particular way, and to postulate an early and widespread authority for them—and then to suggest that the process of New Testament canonization was arbitrary. Orthodox scholars are similarly tempted in their own direction. I know I am. So we are wise to recognize this potential bias in evaluating any argument. But in the end, we still have to make arguments based on history, not on silence.

I don't know the personal story of the other scholars who argue for a vital and early Gnosticism in the church. It really doesn't matter. They might want to argue that Gnosticism should have won the day, or that the church today should resurrect Gnosticism as a valid Christian expression. But their attempt to show that the process of forming the New Testament was somehow arbitrary and manipulative is a failure, and it seems to be driven by something other than historical scholarship.

Ben Witherington III is professor of New Testament at Asbury Theological Seminary and author of many books, including What Have They Done with Jesus? *and* The Gospel Code. *You can learn more about Dr. Witherington at his Web site, www.benwitherington.com. "Why the 'Lost Gospels' Lost Out" was first published in* Christianity Today, *June 2004, Page 26 and is used by permission from Ben Witherington III.*

GNOSTICISM UNMASKED

by D. Jeffrey Bingham

The label "Gnosticism" is a fuzzy one, describing diverse sects and ideas in the ancient world. This chart summarizes those elements within various Gnostic groups that the majority of Christians found especially troublesome. A particular Gnostic sect would not necessarily have held all of the following beliefs.

GNOSTIC VIEW

God: There are two opposing Gods: the supreme, spiritual, unknown Father who is distant from the world and revealed only by Christ; and the subordinate, ignorant, and evil creator of the world (Demiurge).

World: The material world crafted by the Demiurge is evil and keeps the spiritual ones from perfection. It must perish and be escaped.

Humanity: The Gnostics are by nature the elite, spiritual ones, for they have the "seed" of the spiritual realm inside them. This divine spark (the spirit) is trapped within the material, fleshly body and yearns for release from this evil dungeon.

Salvation: Only the immortal spirit of the Gnostic is saved as it gains release from material captivity and returns to the Father's spiritual realm. Salvation is by knowledge (*gnosis*)—by knowing that the true God is the Father, not the Demiurge, and that the true home of the spirit is its place of origin, the Father's realm, not the material world with its bodies of flesh.

Christ: Christ is a spiritual, divine being from the Father's realm who comes to the world to reveal the Father and the true identity of the spiritual ones, the Gnostics. Christ did not become incarnate or suffer on the cross. Instead, he either merely seemed to be human or temporarily inhabited a human being named "Jesus."

Canon and History: There are gospels and testimonies of the apostles that convey the perfect revelation of Christ in addition to (and in some ways superior to) the church's four gospels. This revelation brought by Christ manifests the true knowledge of the Father and the Gnostics, while the Law and the Prophets manifest the Demiurge.

ORTHODOX CHRISTIAN VIEW (as expressed by Irenaeus of Lyons)

God: There is only one true God who is the Creator of the world and the Father of Jesus Christ.

World: The material world was created good by God. It will someday be renewed and made into a fit home for the redeemed.

Humanity: God created all human beings as a union of body and spirit. We are not spiritual by nature —this is a gift available to all by faith through the ministry of the Holy Spirit.

Salvation: Both the immaterial and material aspects of God's creation are saved. By faith in Jesus Christ, a person receives the Holy Spirit who provides spiritual life, resurrects their flesh to eternal life, and redeems the created world.

Christ: Jesus Christ is the one and only Savior, the eternal Son of God made flesh, who truly suffered for the sins of humanity and was truly raised in immortal, incorruptible flesh for their resurrection to eternal life.

Canon and History: The church recognizes only four gospels, Matthew, Mark, Luke, and John, and believes that these four, along with the rest of the New Testament, are in harmony with the Law and the Prophets. All witness to the one true Creator and Father, his Son Jesus Christ, and the Holy Spirit.

D. Jeffrey Bingham is Department Chair and Professor of Theological Studies at Dallas Theological Seminary and is the author of many books including Pocket History of the Church. *"Gnosticism Unmasked" was first published in* Christian History & Biography, *June 30, 2008.*

Open Up

Select one of these activities to launch your discussion time.

Option 1

Discuss these icebreaker questions:

- In our culture, there are many various understandings of who Jesus was. What are some of the various perspectives of Jesus you've seen in our culture? How would some of your non-Christian friends describe Jesus?
- Imagine a conversation with someone you know whose view of Jesus differs significantly from yours. What would you most want to communicate about Jesus? How do you think you'd respond to their take on Jesus's identity and traits?

- A key idea of Gnosticism is that humans have the "divine spark" within them. What are some modern versions of this idea? How have you seen this or other Gnostic ideas in pop culture (movies, TV, books, and so on)?

Option 2

Watch a short clip from the movie *The Da Vinci Code.* In this clip, the fictional character Teabing provides a revisionist version of church history that mirrors the ideology put forth by most real neo-Gnostics today.

Start the clip at approximately 1:01:30 (based on 0:00:00 at studio logo) when Teabing says, "The good book did not arrive by facsimile from heaven." Stop the scene when Teabing says, "As long as there has been one true God, there has been killing in his name" at approximately 1:04:35.

Discuss your thoughts:

- What's your reaction to this depiction of the early church? What bothers you most about Teabing's neo-Gnostic presentation of church history? Why?
- Do you know people who view the church's history this way? Or people whose beliefs have been shaped by books like *The Da Vinci Code?* What attracts them to this type of revisionist history?

■ The Issue

Review the description of Gnostic beliefs in "Gnosticism Unmasked."

- Which aspects of Gnostic teachings are appealing? Why do you think people today are attracted to ideas based on Gnosticism?

The reemergence of Gnostic teaching in modern life can be traced to the recent discovery of Gnostic manuscripts once thought to be the "lost books of the Bible." In December 1945, an Arab peasant found a red earthenware jar near Nag Hammadi, a city in Upper Egypt. Inside the jar were thirteen leather-bound papyrus books, dating from approximately AD 350. According to some scholars, these manuscripts were penned mostly by Jesus's disciples and hence carry their names, such as the Gospel of Thomas, the Gospel of Philip, and the Gospel of Judas. The complete collection was not made available in a popular format in English until 1977. They were released as a collection under the title *The Nag Hammadi Library* and a revised edition was published in 1988.

One influential scholar, Elaine Pagels, who won the National Book Critics Award for her best-selling book *The Gnostic Gospels*, believes that Gnosticism should be considered at least as legitimate as orthodox Christianity. But should these documents be on par with orthodox Christian doctrine? At its core, the debate calls into question whether the Gnostic gospels are in fact historically accurate and compatible with the biblical canon as we know it.

- What difference does it make whether the Gnostic gospels are authentic or not? Do you think the fact that they are ancient manuscripts gives them value even if Jesus's disciples did not write them? Explain your answer.

Reflect

Take a moment to read Luke 1:1–4, John 1:1–5, Romans 3:10–24 and 1 Corinthians 15:1–8 in order to familiarize yourself with these texts. Take notes about what you observe. How do these passages give you confidence in the validity of the biblical gospel message? What are the key points of the authors here? How might these relate to popular ideas in our culture that are derived from Gnosticism?

Let's Explore

The early church rejected the Gnostic gospels for good reason.

Contrary to the discussions in books like the *Da Vinci Code*, the key tenants of Christianity weren't formed hundreds of years after Christ by men seeking positions of power. In fact, there is ample evidence from early Christian documents that there existed a single orthodox Christian faith from the very beginning. In numerous places in the New Testament there are warnings to the early church to reject false teaching and hold to sound doctrine. On one hand, this clearly indicates that the early church teachers were very concerned about fighting against ideas that were not compatible with their doctrine. But it also shows that there *was* a discernable Christian orthodoxy in the early, first-century church, long before Gnosticism took hold or the Gnostic gospels were written.

Read Paul's succinct summary of the gospel message in 1 Corinthians 15:1–8 written around AD 55.

- How does Paul's explanation of the gospel contrast with the tenants of Gnosticism? Similarly, how does it contrast with ideas about Christ and Christianity commonly held in today's culture? Be specific.

- What significance do you find in the fact that early Christians had an established orthodoxy *before* the Gnostic gospels were written? What implications does this have for our faith today?

Christianity is based upon historical fact. Its claims are rooted in actual events, not just ideas; in people who lived in time and space, not just principles; in revelation, not speculation; in incarnation, not abstraction. Historical accuracy was of prime importance to Luke, who wrote the gospel known by his name.

Read Luke 1:1–4.

- What is the significance of Luke's account of Jesus's life? What difference does it make that he took great care to record the events in an orderly fashion and base it on firsthand testimony?

- What do you think it means when we say Christianity is based upon actual events and not simply ideas?

- Why doesn't the discovery of the Gnostic gospels tell us anything more about the historic Jesus? How might you answer this question if posed to you by a Christian who felt confused by what he or she has heard about these "lost gospels"?

Gnostic writings contradict biblical doctrine.

The gospels of the Nag Hammadi library present a view of the world at extreme odds with the one found in the Old and New Testaments. The Gnostic gospels, as the editorial states, "were rejected precisely because they had rejected the Christian continuity with historic Jewish faith."

For starters, Gnosticism posits that an all-good or powerful God did not create the universe. According to the Gospel of Philip, the world as we know it is really a mistake. The creator of the universe supposedly bungled the act of creation, and as a result, the material cosmos is filled with pain, decay, and death. The record of God's creation from Genesis 1:31 stands in stark contrast to this botched view of creation. God pronounces his work of creation as "very good."

Read Romans 3:10–24.

- Why is it important to understand that it was *man's* choice to turn away from God, thus causing the pain, decay, and death we know in this world? How would your faith in God be different if you viewed him as somehow flawed, imperfect, or finite?

Another crucial difference between Gnosticism and Christianity concerns the identity and purpose of Jesus's life. According to Gnostic teaching, Jesus was neither God nor man, and his main purpose was not to save us from sin but to come as a guide to open access to spiritual understanding. But Jesus's deity is clearly seen in numerous passages in the New Testament.

Read John 1:1–5.

- Why do you think it is popular in contemporary culture to reduce Jesus to the status of a human prophet or teacher but deny his divinity? What are the implications for those who separate these two integral parts of his nature?

The Gospel of Judas is particularly interesting because it states that Judas was not the traitor that orthodox Christians have assumed all these years. Rather, he was Jesus's most trusted disciple, because it was through his betrayal that Jesus was able to go to the cross. According to the story, Jesus actually gave Judas the task of betraying him so that, through death, he could be freed from his physical body. (Gnostics believe that matter, including the physical body, is evil.) So Judas was actually a hero.

- Assume for the moment that the Gospel of Judas is accurate in its portrayal of Judas as a hero who helped Jesus on his path to the cross. Does this dramatic reversal of motives on Judas's part change the biblical account of Jesus's sacrifice on the cross? Why or why not?

We are special, not because of our knowledge of self, but because we are created by God.

Gnosticism claims that some people are special because they have the potential to understand spiritual secrets others cannot. And the greatest spiritual insight is not knowledge of God, as Christianity would profess, but rather knowing *oneself* at a deep level. In other words, self-knowledge *is* knowledge of god; the self and the divine are identical. This helps us to understand how Gnosticism got its name. The Greek word *gnosis* means knowledge.

- How can the search for self-knowledge become an end in itself? What can happen to one's faith when self-betterment becomes the primary goal?

- On the other hand, in what ways do you see self-knowledge and self-awareness as positive attributes through which Christians can benefit? Where would you draw the line between healthy self-awareness and Gnostic ideas in modern forms?

A knowledge and awareness of our thoughts, emotions, and behavior can be beneficial in our daily lives. But it is not an end in itself as proclaimed through the Gnostic writings. We don't have this capacity for self-knowledge because we are one of the enlightened ones, as Gnosticism would claim. We have been given some degree of self-knowledge because we are created in God's image (Genesis 1:26–27). We are special because God has called us so. Self-knowledge, in its proper function, is to recognize our status as created beings and our need to bow before our Creator. Gnosticism believes that humans need to be liberated from their human limitations. Christianity calls us to embrace our humanity and live faithfully in submission to God and his plan for our lives.

Going Forward

Form pairs to read this quotation and discuss these final questions:

What is truly at stake in the debate over the Gnostic gospels is whether they meet the test of being reliable and therefore trustworthy. F. F. Bruce, in his classic work *The New Testament Documents: Are They Reliable?* (Eerdmans, 2003), asks that fundamental question in the opening line of his preface. He later amplifies what the answer implies by saying:

> The historical "once-for-all-ness" of Christianity, which distinguishes it from those religions and philosophical systems which are not specifically related to any particular time, makes the reliability of the writings, which purport to record this revelation, a question of first-rate importance.

If Christianity is judged by its historical accuracy, then a competing viewpoint (like the gospels of Nag Hammadi) must be judged by the same standard if it is to be taken seriously.

- How would you assess the modern-day church in terms of how concerned it is about issues like the validity of the Gnostic gospels or their influence in society? How might the church more adequately address these issues?

- How can *you* be a standard-bearer for the true historical Jesus in light of the popular acceptance of Gnostic ideas such as those presented in *The Da Vinci Code* or the work of Elaine Pagels?

- What do you think is most important to communicate to friends who may be influenced by Gnostic tenets?

Gather back together and use the "Orthodox Christian View" section of "Unmasking Gnosticism" to guide a time of concluding prayer. Worship and praise God for the truths highlighted in the article and affirm together your belief in the key tenets of the gospel message.

Notes

What do these oft-overlooked books say about the brutal and seductive world into which Jesus was born?

SCRIPTURE FOCUS

- Exodus 20:1, 22; 21:1
- Malachi 4:5–6
- Matthew 11:10
- John 1:1–18

SESSION 7

LESSONS FROM THE APOCRYPHA

■

Ever heard a sermon based on 1 Maccabees? Ever meditated on a passage from Tobit? Have you ever even *heard* of 1 Maccabees or Tobit?

These books, along with others such as Judith, Baruch, 1 and 2 Esdras, and others, were considered part of the biblical canon up until the Reformation. They're part of the Apocrypha (which means "hidden") and are published in Catholic Bibles, Greek Orthodox Bibles, and recently as an appendix in some Protestant Bibles as well. So why don't Protestants consider these books to be part of Scripture? *Should* they be? What value, if any, might they have in the lives of evangelicals?

This study explores the history of the Apocrypha, then asks what Christians can learn from first-century Jews.

Before You Meet

Read "Brief History of the Apocrypha" by Elesha Coffman from *Christianity Today*.

BRIEF HISTORY OF THE APOCRYPHA

by Elesha Coffman

Jewish leaders approved the final makeup of the Hebrew Bible at the Council of Jamnia in AD 90. They included all of the texts that are in the Protestant Old Testament, but excluded a number of texts that were a part of the Septuagint—a Greek translation of the Hebrew Law and the Prophets, as well as a few other books. This decision did not, however, send these extra texts to the dustbin. They lived on and were used by a variety of people, including early Christians.

For a while, the Christian community made no hard-and-fast decisions regarding the canon. The Septuagint was the predominant "Old Testament" version that Christians used. The Christian canon also included, depending on where you lived, texts that are now included in the New Testament as well as many texts that have since been lost. The texts were neither universally available nor uniformly emphasized.

Imagine that, instead of a hardbound Bible, a pastor had a stack of purportedly scriptural pamphlets that had arrived in the mail. The pamphlets came in sets that sometimes overlapped and sometimes differed. Not all of the pamphlets were in the same language or of the same quality. When the pastor was not sure which of the pamphlets to trust, he could ask his local colleagues, but he had little idea which texts pastors were using two hundred miles away. That was more or less the situation in the first three centuries after Christ. Even what we now call the New Testament was not determined until three or four centuries after Christ's death and resurrection.

Inevitably, conflicts arose. Church leaders in different geographic areas could not agree upon which texts should be included in the Christian Scriptures. The result was a proliferation of canons, including the Ethiopian Orthodox (eighty-one books), the Syrian (sixty-one books), and the Latin (seventy-three books). The last of these became the official canon of the Western (Roman) church and is still used by Roman Catholics.

Centuries later, during the Renaissance and Reformation, some scholars began to question the inclusion of the books we call the Apocrypha in the Western Bible. One argument said these books were not included in the Hebrew canon, determined in AD 90. In addition, men like John Wycliffe, William Tyndale, and Martin Luther no longer trusted church tradition, which had become a principle argument for keeping the books of the Apocrypha.

Nonetheless, early Protestants retained the Apocrypha in their Bibles (including the King James Version) but assigned it secondary status. In time, they dropped it entirely. Some Protestants came to consider the Apocrypha not just unscriptural, but spiritually unhealthy. This stemmed mainly from the Protestants' desire to distance themselves from Roman Catholics, but also because the Apocrypha contains the only explicit references to purgatory.

Elesha Coffman is a graduate student in religion at Duke University. She was formerly the managing editor of Christian History *magazine. This brief history first appeared in an earlier version of the Current Issues Bible Study "Lessons from the Apocrypha" available for download from www.christianbiblestudies.com.*

■ Open Up

Select one of these activities to launch your discussion time.

Option 1

Discuss these icebreaker questions:

- Which book of the Bible are you *most* familiar with (from reading, sermons, etc.)? Which book of the Bible do you feel *least* familiar with?
- Can you name all the books of the Bible? Can you name all (or any) of the books of the Apocrypha? Demonstrate it.

- Do you own a Bible that includes the Apocrypha? Have you ever read anything from it? Explain your familiarity—or lack of familiarity—with the Apocrypha.

Option 2

If most of your group members aren't familiar with the Apocrypha or haven't read any Apocryphal texts, take five to ten minutes to learn more about the various texts online.

Some interesting web sites summarizing the content of the Apocrypha are:

Catholic Encyclopedia's description of the books of the Apocrypha, available at http://www.newadvent.org/cathen/01601a.htm

Wikipedia's description of the texts included in various historical Bibles, available at http://en.wikipedia.org/wiki/Biblical_apocrypha

Peruse some of the actual text of the Apocrypha by using the search engine available at http://bible.oremus.org/

The Issue

Renovaré, the spiritual formation ministry founded by writer and speaker Richard Foster, decided to include the Apocrypha in their *Renovaré Spiritual Formation Bible* (Zondervan). Foster explained their reasoning to CT this way:

> We discussed it a lot. Most of the church throughout most of her history has had those writings, and we felt we should follow that. The early church had the Septuagint, which had essentially the Apocrypha in it. The great Christian traditions—Orthodox, Catholic, Anglican, and many other groups—have used the Apocrypha. To describe it, we use the word *deuterocanonical,* which means "second canon."
>
> None of these groups have ever accorded the Apocrypha or the deuterocanonicals the same authority as Scripture; neither do we. But they have viewed it as really good literature that fills an important historical gap from Malachi to Matthew. To understand how Jesus was speaking into his day, you have to understand the deuterocanonical literature. Even the

Reformers like Luther said it was good to read. ("Not a Hallmark Bible," September 2005)

- What's your reaction to the idea of the Apocrypha being included in a Bible primarily for Protestants?

■ Reflect

Take a moment to read Exodus 20:1, 22; 21:1; Malachi 4:5–6; Matthew 11:10; and John 1:1–18. Familiarize yourself with the main ideas in each text; take notes about your observations and any questions these passages raise for you.

■ Let's Explore

Where did the Apocrypha come from?

We know from both scholars and hints in the biblical texts that what is now called the Old Testament (or the Hebrew Bible) slowly took shape as new pieces were written and added or rejected. The most sacred, most important texts became fixed as the *canon*, a word that means "rule" or "code of law." You could draw a rough parallel to the U.S. Constitution, the rule by which all other American laws are judged.

Some texts earned an automatic place in the canon. For example, no one ever questioned the canonicity of Exodus 20–23, the bedrock of Jewish law.

Other texts did not make the cut. The Old Testament refers to some of these texts; The Book of Jashar (see 2 Samuel 1:18) and the book of the kings of Judah and Israel (see 2 Chron. 16:11), for instance, were obviously important in their day, but Jewish leaders did not deem it necessary to preserve them forever. Possibly these texts were never even copied.

The texts of the Apocrypha fit somewhere in the middle; they must have been highly esteemed, because they were copied frequently in the centuries before and after Jesus's birth. Still, the apocryphal texts never made it into the Protestant canon.

- Step back into history and imagine what criteria you might have used to determine which texts were divinely inspired (and thus should be part of the canon) and which text should not be included. What factors would you consider?

- Imagine the texts of Old Testament-period books such as the Book of Jashar or the book of the kings of Judah and Israel were found in an archeological dig. Would you want to read them? Would you consider them part of Scripture? Would you want them included in your Bible? Explain.

- In your opinion, what makes the Apocrypha different than other ancient extra-biblical writings such as the Gnostic gospels? Or do you regard it the same way as texts such as the Gospel of Judas?

Many Jews believe that God stopped speaking through prophets around 400 BC. Even the author of 1 Maccabees, writing more than one hundred years before Jesus's birth, acknowledges, "There had not been such great distress in Israel since the time prophets ceased to appear among the people" (1 Macc. 9:27, NAB). The last Old Testament prophet, Malachi, ended his book with the promise that Elijah would return to speak for God again (Malachi 4:5–6). Many Jews still wait for this event.

According to Jesus, John the Baptist fulfilled Malachi's prophecy. Read aloud Malachi 4:5–6 and Matthew 11:10.

Jesus did not, however, identify any prophets between Malachi and John the Baptist. This is one reason why Protestants don't view as Scripture any texts written during those centuries.

- If Jesus had referred to texts from the Apocrypha, would that change your opinion about them? Why or why not?

If the Apocrypha isn't Scripture, why should we care about it?

- In what ways have you learned about the culture and historical events of Jesus's time (such as through sermons, movies, or reading)? How has that information provided new insights for you about biblical accounts of Jesus's teachings? Give examples.

In a *Christianity Today* article called "Violent Night, Holy Night" Tim Stafford offers at least three reasons evangelicals should care about the Apocrypha. One, the Apocrypha helps us understand the world into which

Jesus was born—a world more like the modern Middle East than like an idyllic Christmas pageant. Two, the Apocrypha illustrates what kind of savior first-century Jews were looking for—someone very unlike Jesus. Three, the Apocrypha gets inside the mind of an insular, defensive culture that located evil "out there" instead of "in here." In this, the Apocrypha shows that first-century Judaism and twenty-first-century American Christianity share a dangerous trait.

- Which of Stafford's reasons for caring about the Apocrypha do you find most compelling? What might you add to the list?

In the absence of prophets who speak for God, the Apocrypha contains examples of heroes, most notably Judas Maccabeus, "an outstanding general who led his outnumbered army to victory upon victory." During Jesus's lifetime, many zealots were hoping for a similar hero—a Messiah who'd liberate the Jews from political oppression.

- In what ways did Jesus fulfill this hope for a hero? How did he contrast with it?

Explore Stafford's three reasons further by reading John 1:1–18. Consider each phrase against the backdrop of the Apocrypha and what you've learned about the cultural and historical context of Jesus's life.

- How do the phrases and ideas in this passage take on new significance?

After you've discussed the question above, consider these insights drawn from the Apocrypha's depiction of the culture and history of the time.

John 1:5—First-century Israel was a very dark, oppressive place; darkness existed not only in the hearts of the ruling pagans but also in the hearts of the Jews.

John 1:7—John the Baptist reinstated the long-vacant office of prophet.

John 1:9—Israel's "us versus them" attitude contradicted God's plan which was for the light to be available to every man.

John 1:14—The time, place, and cultural/historical setting of Jesus's birth matter a great deal to our understanding of Jesus's teachings and his life.

John 1:17—Unlike the grace and truth brought by Christ, the heroes of the Apocrypha brought very different things: new rules and ceremonies, military glory, political liberation, reinforcement of in-group mentality. Compared to these gifts, grace and truth seemed like a let-down.

- What would you like to learn more about when it comes to the political and cultural climate of the first century? What steps do you want to take to learn more and enhance your reading of Scripture?

■ Going Forward

In "Between Malachi and Matthew" in *Books & Culture,* Ken Stewart comments on the reemergence of interest in the Apocrypha among some evangelicals, saying,

> [One reason for the interest] would be the suspicion among many younger evangelicals that our tradition has delivered to us a "stripped down" version of historic Christianity. Everyone knows some evangelical

who has investigated and then put down roots in the Episcopal, Catholic, or Orthodox expression of the Christian faith on the basis of this sense of feeling "shortchanged." Some have felt shortchanged as to reverential styles of worship, emphasis on creeds and confessions, and the loss of the conception of "one holy Catholic church."

- What's your response to this quote? Can you relate to these reasons for interest in the Apocrypha? Why or why not?

Stewart then cautions,

> But before we hurry out and replace the Bibles we have, which likely contain no Apocrypha, with those that do, let us remember that from antiquity, the Christian thinkers who have labored hardest to read Hebrew and to dialogue with Jewish scholars have been the most resolute in cautioning us against making more of the Apocrypha than what they are: a collection of intertestamental writings of mixed quality and accuracy—yet which shed interesting and valuable light on the centuries between Malachi and John the Baptist.

There are many texts competing for Scriptural status today, from the Gnostic gospels to the *Book of Mormon*. Because of its inclusion in their Bibles, some Christians view the Apocrypha as on par with Scripture.

- Is this perspective on the Apocrypha dangerous? How might you respond to a Christian who asserts that evangelicals, on the other hand, are missing out on biblical history by dismissing the Apocrypha?

- After this discussion, do you plan on reading some of the Apocrypha? Why or why not? In what other ways might you supplement your reading of Scripture in order to better understand its historical context?

Pray together, focusing on praising God for his Word and asking God for wisdom and discernment as you continue to explore Scripture together.

How can we get the most from God's Word?

SCRIPTURE FOCUS

Psalm 119:89–114

Philippians 1–4

SESSION 8

LISTENING TO GOD IN SCRIPTURE

"Many of us do not know how to listen to the voice of God in Scripture, because we were trained to view the Bible as a series of verses strung together like pearls on a string, each having its own meaning in itself. We were trained to resort to that treasure trove whenever we felt a need for something from it, plucking the gem that satisfies our quest at the moment," says John H. Stek in "Interrogating the Bible."

How *should* we approach Scripture? Is there a right way and a wrong way? What are the best methods of reading and understanding God's Word? How can Christians remain open to God's message while studying Scripture? This study will challenge us to think about these issues.

Before You Meet

Read "Interrogating the Bible" from *Christianity Today.*

INTERROGATING THE BIBLE

It's supposed to be the other way around.

by John H. Stek

Some years ago, a father of ten children deserted his family to become an evangelist. His warrant for doing so? Luke 14:26 KJV: "If any man come to me, and hate not his father, and mother, and wife, and children, and brethren, and sisters, yea, and his own life also, he cannot be my disciple."

The man had obviously isolated this verse from the whole of Luke's testimony and so had convinced himself of the rightness of an action Jesus would have abhorred.

I have seen a condolence card that does less damage but betrays the same misuse of Scripture. It quotes Job 11:16–18 under the heading "To Comfort You": "You will surely forget your trouble, recalling it only as waters gone by . . ." The promise has the ring of comfort until you read the rest of the passage. It is part of Zophar's not-so-subtle accusation: "If you put away the sin that is in your hand and allow no evil to dwell in your tent, then . . ." (v. 14 NIV).

The Voice of God

Many of us do not know how to listen to the voice of God in Scripture, because we were trained to view the Bible as a series of verses strung together like pearls on a string, each having its own meaning in itself. We were trained to resort to that treasure trove whenever we felt a need for something from it, plucking the gem that satisfies our quest at the moment.

Ideally, we respond receptively to God's message. But usually we do not come to the Word ready to listen. Isolated verses have become "God's will" for us in the circumstances, or they serve as magic words that we use on God to try to manipulate him, or as levers that we employ to get what we want from God.

When this is done to rationalize hate-filled motives, the gospel itself is violated. But even when it is done with good intentions, we hamper ourselves from truly hearing God's Word. Ironically, a long-standing tradition in Bible publishing and certain popular Christian practices have contributed to this "string of pearls" notion of the Bible.

About the time of the Reformation, with its great renewal in Bible study, a numerical grid of chapters and verses was imposed on the biblical text for the sole purpose of facilitating quick and accurate reference. Unfortunately, this tool eventually created misunderstanding. Many who did not know the origin and purpose of the chapter and verse numbers got the impression that they belonged to the original manuscripts and indicated actual units of composition.

When Bible publishers began printing each verse as a paragraph, readers were further misled into believing that each verse is self-contained. These editorial and layout judgments—originally made at a publishing house and then perpetuated through publishing tradition—have contributed to incorrect notions about the text.

Interrogating the Bible

Some common practices of pastors and Christian teachers have probably had even more impact in creating the "string of pearls" view: the widespread practice of preaching on a single verse, creating devotional readings that jump off from a verse for the day, memorizing individual verses in Sunday school, devising Bible studies that move through the text verse by verse as if each were a separate unit for study, and studying the Bible topically.

Single-verse memorization has contributed to the problem by giving both Christians and cultists handy tools for propping up their preconceptions. "The truth shall make you free" (John 8:32) is one of the most widely quoted lines in the Bible. I have heard it quoted by sectarians, claiming that their particular notions are the "truth" that sets people free. I have even heard it on the lips of agnostics, asserting that science provides the "truth" that frees people from the shackles of religion.

And the well-known proverb, "Train up a child in the way he should go; and when he is old, he will not depart from it" (Prov. 22:6), has troubled many godly parents. They forget that it comes from Proverbs, and understand it as though it came from the Law or the Prophets. They mistakenly hear the "Train . . ." clause as a commandment and the "when he is old . . ." clause as a prophecy. They forget that as a proverb this verse offers godly counsel that adults usually reflect the training they received as children.

Topical study has also been enormously influential. "What does the Bible say about . . ." is the way people often come to Scripture. They use a concordance to find biblical references to the topic under investigation. Then the verses supposedly pertaining to the topic are plucked from their contexts and assembled, and conclusions are drawn.

The misuse of Bible dictionaries and encyclopedias and topical study aids such as chain-reference Bibles has contributed to the problem. Most theological books are also topically oriented.

Theologians want to present what the Bible says about the Trinity, providence, or whatever their special interest is. Having used the topical method of interrogating the Bible, they furnish "proof texts" to warrant their theological assertions. Thus a topical grid as artificial as the numerical one is imposed on the Bible—often with the same misleading results.

We rightly view the Bible as an authoritative book, offering us knowledge of God and his will. But we then tend to use it as we use other authoritative texts, such as the *Encyclopædia Britannica,* rather than as a unified narrative of the story of salvation.

Are we interested in information on drunkenness? We turn topically to *Bartlett's Familiar Quotations* to find what various wits have uttered. We turn topically to *Roget's Thesaurus* to find synonyms *crude* and *clever*. We turn topically to the *Merck Manual* to discover alcoholism's physical symptoms and some suggested treatments. And we turn to a Bible concordance to find God's opinion on drink and drunks. But the result of topical investigation is that the authentic message of the Bible's authors is sometimes suppressed.

We Set the Agenda

Every time we turn to Scripture to ask, "What does the Bible say about . . ." (and almost every time a preacher searches the Bible for "a text about . . .") *we* set the agenda for Scripture's speaking. We raise the questions. We control the dialog, allowing the Word of God to speak only to our momentary interests. We do not shut our mouths before God and open our hearts to listen to what God's Spirit has to say to us.

We can also silence Scripture by the counterfeit kind of listening practiced in too many Bible study groups. I read a verse (or a few verses) and ask myself (or someone else): "What does that verse say to you—right now as you hear it?" Most answers provide little more than data for a psychological study of the answerer. The verse triggers in the hearer an association or a whole cluster of associations that reveal more of the respondent than of the Spirit. Our spirits speak, and the Spirit of God is shut off.

I sometimes ask my students in a seminary course on the Former Prophets, "For what might you turn to the Book of Joshua?" The responses usually include "to find out what the Bible has to say about war"; "to learn the boundaries of the various Israelite tribes"; "to read about the life of Joshua"; "to find illustrations of the sovereign working of God"; "to glean some biblical examples of obedience and disobedience and their consequences."

Indeed, one can find in Joshua materials in some way relevant to these questions. But to assume that the author wrote Joshua to serve such purposes is for the reader to control the Bible's speaking. To use Joshua in this manner is indeed to *use* it, not to listen to it.

I then ask my students to do something shocking in its simplicity. I tell them to read Joshua from beginning to end in one sitting, to listen closely as the author weaves his narrative, to note how his story begins and how it ends, to pay close attention to the episodes he includes and how each of them contributes to the outcome, to observe the narrator's art and the subtle clues he gives to his message, to consider at each stage of reading what the author perceives to be at stake.

I advise them that if they would be hearers of the Word they must let the author of Joshua have his whole say before they presume to know whereof he speaks. And they must all the while be silent and open, letting the author lead them where he will. They must not try to anticipate what he will say. (Preachers who rummage through the Bible to find texts on which to hang topical or biographical sermons are often guilty of substituting their word for the biblical Word. That such erroneously conceived sermons may motivate people to do good is not an argument against the patient listening to Scripture. Instead, it only confirms an old Dutch proverb that "God can strike a straight blow even with a crooked stick.")

The translators and editors of most contemporary translations of the Bible seek to achieve a style and layout that invites extended reading of the Bible. As one of the translators of the New International Version, I hoped that many readers would do what they had never done before, namely, read even the longer books of the Bible in one sitting—especially the narrative books (including Job), the Epistles, and Revelation. Only thus would they be reading these books as the authors intended.

To be sure, after a thorough reading of a book, one may focus on smaller passages for close study, meditation, and memorization. Afterward, one may come with questions. Afterward, one may assemble "what Scripture has to say about . . ." But one should do all this only after having heard the authors out. Let the authors of Scripture set the agenda.

Should no study aids be used—Bible dictionaries, encyclopedias, concordances, commentaries, study Bibles? Surely they should. But they are to be aids for informed reading. They may not, they cannot, become substitutes. There can be no topical summaries that can serve in place of the Bible—not even if the topics assembled are all "theological." Whatever study tools one employs, they must be used solely to illumine "what the Spirit has to say to the churches" (Rev. 2–3) through the biblical texts.

Too often we have interrogated the Bible. Too often we have used the Bible. If we would hear the voice of God, we must assume the attitude, and learn the art, of listening to the text the way the authors wrote it.

John Stek served as a professor of Old Testament, Calvin Theological Seminary, Grand Rapids, Michigan for thirty years. He was a member of the translation committee for the New International Version *and an associate editor of* The NIV Study Bible. *"Interrogating the Bible" was first published in* Christianity Today.

Open Up

Select one of these activities to launch your discussion time.

Option 1

Discuss these icebreaker questions:

- Have you ever had a time in your life when you felt that you clearly "heard" from God? If so, describe it. How did God communicate to you? What was God's message for you?
- Imagine you could hear from God clearly, directly, and concretely *right now*—a message from God specifically for you. What would you most want to hear from God about? Why?
- Now consider the question differently: What do you imagine God might most want to communicate to you about? How might God's perspective on what you need to hear be different from what you most desire to hear?

Option 2

Take time to reflect on all you've discussed and explored over the past seven studies by turning household items into symbols together. Bring odd, unique, or everyday household objects, such as a light bulb, a garlic press, a hammer, a pillow, and so on. Put all the objects in the center of the room, then take turns selecting an object and using it to share a personal reflection point about God's Word. For example, someone might select a pillow and say: "Lately God's Word has been a comfort to me—a source of peace and calm amid the stressful situations I'm facing at work."

Be creative, have fun, and think out of the box—you'll be surprised by what you come up with together!

The Issue

There are many different avenues by which Christians approach Scripture, including topical studies; verse-by-verse study; use of Bible study guides or video courses; Bible verse memory; inductive Bible study; short devotional readings; praying a passage of Scripture; study enhanced with research tools like concordances, commentaries, and Bible dictionaries; and more.

- Which of these approaches to Scripture have you experienced? Which do you feel most familiar with or enjoy the most? Why?

In "Interrogating the Bible," John Stek is critical of some Bible study methods that are popular today particularly because they promote a way of reading Scripture that's much different than the original authors intended.

- What was your initial reaction to Stek's comments? In your opinion, what are the strengths or weaknesses of his argument?

Reflect

Take a moment to read Psalm 119:89–114. Take notes recording your initial reaction to this text. Jot down key words, important phrases, or questions this passage raises for you.

■ Let's Explore

Our understanding of Scripture is enriched when we approach each book as a whole rather than as a collection of independent sentences.

Stek opens his article with the painful example of a father abandoning his family because he took a verse of Scripture out of context. The man had obviously isolated this verse from the whole of Luke's testimony and so had convinced himself of the rightness of an action Jesus would have abhorred.

Read Philippians 4:13. This verse is frequently quoted by Christians in a variety of situations and often with different understandings of what it means. The first part of the verse is often quoted in secular culture too: "I can do all things!"

- How have you heard this verse used or quoted? What interpretations (or misinterpretations) do people often have of this verse? What are some other examples you've seen or heard of people taking Scripture passages out of context? How do you think the Apostle Paul would react?

Now read the passage in context, either by reading the entire brief epistle aloud together (Philippians 1–4) or, if you have less time, reading all of Philippians 4.

- What new insights does the context provide for Paul's intentions with this verse? What nuances does the surrounding text provide for your understanding of "do all things" (vs. 13)?

Stek critiques the piece-meal approach to Scripture that views "the Bible as a series of verses strung together like pearls on a string, each having its own meaning in itself."

- Do you think it's *wrong* to select individual verses as "pearls"? For example, can Philippians 4:13 be properly understood on its own, apart from the surrounding paragraphs? Defend your view.

Our understanding of Scripture is enriched when we pay attention to the author's voice and to the particularities of a book's genre.

- When you read secular texts for pleasure or study (such as novels, sports magazines, news articles, or poetry), how do you approach them differently? What expectations do you bring to various genres? For example, what do you expect from a history book that may be different than what you'd expect from reading a poem? Provide a personal example.

The books of the Bible contain a variety of genres, including historical narrative, law, poetry, prophecy, Gospel, and epistle (letter). The epistles were meant to be read aloud to the churches who received them. With this historical and cultural setting in mind, it's hard to imagine the first hearers isolating one sentence from the rest. (After all, we'd hardly expect someone to fixate on just one sentence of an email we've sent!) It's also hard to imagine the first hearers losing sight of the text's genre: a letter with timely, pertinent, God-inspired words for them written by someone they knew and loved. The first hearers would have had Paul in mind, understanding the text not as a message directly to them from God but rather as God's message to them through the words of their beloved brother Paul.

- Briefly discuss how we should approach each of the biblical genres listed above. What should we expect from each particular type of writing? What *shouldn't* we expect from various genres?

Our understanding of Scripture is enriched when we listen with our heart and soul as well as our mind.

Read aloud Psalm 119:89–114.

- How would you describe the psalmist's regard for God's Word? How did he *feel* about God's Word? How did he *interact* with God's Word?

Bible study is a very important spiritual discipline. But there are other important approaches to Scripture that are less cerebral and more spirit-oriented, such as *lectio divina* or other forms of Christian meditation and devotional reading.

For example, *lectio divina,* an ancient prayer-focused approach to Scripture, follows four basic steps.

1. *Lectio:* Slowly and purposefully reading a passage of Scripture.
2. *Meditato:* Taking time to think about the passage and ruminate on what it means. Allowing the words and ideas to sink in and listening to the passage's message with a spirit of openness.
3. *Oratio:* Praying in response to the passage, expressing whatever arises in your heart.
4. *Contemplatio:* Resting in quietness, calmly waiting in God's presence; surrendering your will to God's will.

Other forms of spiritual reading (also called devotional reading) include actively imagining what it would be like to be present during a biblical account (such as listening to Jesus teach or watching him heal someone) or praying passages of Scripture.

- With your God-given personality in mind, do you tend to naturally lean more toward intellectual interaction with God's Word (such as Bible study and research) or toward more emotional/spiritual interaction with God's Word (such as spiritual reading and Christian meditation)? Which of these two important areas of Bible learning do you desire to grow in? Explain.

Going Forward

Form pairs to discuss this quote and the final questions.

Stek believes that "[t]oo often we have interrogated the Bible. Too often we have used the Bible." In his view, when we search the Bible for "a text about . . ." we are setting the agenda for the Bible's speaking to us.

- What does it mean to you to allow God to set the agenda for Scripture's message to you rather than setting the agenda yourself? What does this look like in practical terms?

- Compare the way you normally regard Scripture with that of the psalmist in Psalm 119. How do you desire to deepen your own love for God's Word? How do you feel personally challenged? Share a specific commitment you feel prompted to make.

Pray with your partner, asking God to instill in you both a deep and abiding love for his Word. Invite God to guide you in your efforts to both learn from Scripture and be changed it.

CPSIA information can be obtained at www.ICGtesting.com
Printed in the USA
LVOW100527240113

316864LV00011B/57/P

9 781418 534103